*"See what a man can do
when with his spirit he rises like a star . . .
over the dark veil of the world."*

                            Juliusz Słowacki

Discovering the Human Person

In Conversation with John Paul II

Stanisław Grygiel

Translated by
Michelle K. Borras

HUMANUM
PONTIFICAL JOHN PAUL II
INSTITUTE SERIES

WILLIAM B. EERDMANS PUBLISHING COMPANY
GRAND RAPIDS, MICHIGAN / CAMBRIDGE, U.K.

© 2014 Stanisław Grygiel
All rights reserved

Published 2014 by
Wm. B. Eerdmans Publishing Co.
2140 Oak Industrial Drive N.E., Grand Rapids, Michigan 49505 /
P.O. Box 163, Cambridge CB3 9PU U.K.
www.eerdmans.com

Library of Congress Cataloging-in-Publication Data

Grygiel, Stanisław.

Discovering the human person: in conversation with John Paul II /
Stanisław Grygiel; translated by Michelle K. Borras.
pages   cm
Expanded version of the Michael J. McGivney lectures
delivered from March 18 to 21, 2013
at the
John Paul II Institute for Studies on Marriage and Family,
Catholic University of America, Washington, D.C.
ISBN 978-0-8028-7154-1 (pbk.: alk. paper)
1. John Paul II, Pope, 1920-2005.
2. Theological anthropology — Catholic Church.
3. Catholic Church — Doctrines.   I. Title.

BT701.3.G7913   2014
233 — dc23

2014013048

Humanum is an imprint of the John Paul II Institute for Studies on Marriage
and Family at the Catholic University of America in Washington, D.C.

Contents

Foreword, by Carl A. Anderson — vii

Introduction — x

1. *Vir fortis* — 1
2. *Via pulchritudinis — via crucis* — 42
3. The New Evangelization — 83
4. Marriage and the Family — 93
5. Nation and State — 129

Foreword

It is a commonplace today to think of the "John Paul II Generation" as those young men and women who may have participated in a World Youth Day event or have been strongly influenced by the papacy of John Paul II, and who are now entering their professional careers and vocations to religious life or to marriage and family. But the reality is that the "John Paul II Generation" began many years earlier and far from the world's attention with another generation of young adults who gathered around Bishop Karol Wojtyła. This was a generation that listened to him speaking from the pulpit and in the classroom, that shared Sunday-afternoon dinners with him, that walked with him in the forests and in the mountains. He prepared these young adults for marriage, baptized their children, gave them spiritual guidance, and during times of sickness and tragedy offered them consolation. This was a generation that went with him on pilgrimage to places like the Marian shrine at Ludźmierz and stood with him to erect a cross in defiance of communist oppression in the new "churchless" city of Nowa Huta. In this truly extraordinary book, Stanisław Grygiel opens for us a window into the man who inspired this generation, the man whom the world would come to know as Pope John Paul II.

Soon after his election as pope, John Paul II called Professor Grygiel to Rome to serve as one of the founding members of a new pontifical faculty that would be officially established at the Lateran University in 1981. Soon to be known as the John Paul II Institute for Studies on Marriage and Family, it would pioneer a new approach to global theological education. Sessions of the Institute would soon be established, first in Washington, D.C., and then in the years to come on virtually every continent,

Foreword

bringing together scholars from Europe, North and South America, Asia, Africa, and Australia to study the challenges confronting marriage and family from a uniquely global perspective. And yet the Institute, which has now been engaged in this study for over three decades, is unique in another way as well. It is a community of scholars devoted to the study of the human person in all of his dimensions but centered on a study of the person in that community that is the original cell of human society: marriage and the family. From the beginning of this work, Professor Grygiel has been one of its most profound guiding lights. The reasons for this are abundantly evident in the pages that follow — an expanded version of the Fr. Michael McGivney Lectures given in 2013 at the Institute's Washington, D.C., session at the Catholic University of America.

We see here how, while surrounded by the dehumanizing pressures of communist totalitarianism, Karol Wojtyła lived day in and day out a profound Christian personalism. In the midst of constant propaganda about creating a new collectivist, godless society, Karol Wojtyła lived a communion of persons. Over the years, he would invite many others into this communion. In this way, he experienced an authentic freedom and developed what he would describe as an "adequate" understanding of the human person. As Grygiel makes evident in chapter 1, there is nothing abstract or artificial about Wojtyła's view of the person. Karol Wojtyła wrote his anthropology "above all with his life." It is in relationships — especially those open to the possibility of deep personal development — that we are able to realize that we belong to one another and are obliged to care for one another. Thus for Wojtyła, the communion of persons is a place of freedom and a place that exists for freedom. It is the place where "the truth that makes us free" (cf. John 8:32) is revealed. Decades later such an understanding of human solidarity in freedom would change the face of Europe, but its origin could be seen in the faces of those who gathered around Karol Wojtyła years earlier.

Much has been written regarding Karol Wojtyła the artist — about his early experience as an actor in Krakow's Rhapsodic Theater as well as his dedication as a poet and playwright. In chapter 2, Professor Grygiel takes us further by opening a window into Wojtyła's artistic sensibility, revealing its profoundly spiritual nature and showing us how it shaped his philosophical and theological thought. In reading, we come to understand that for Wojtyła, "Every human being is called to make of himself a work of art on earth." We cannot help but think of Dostoevsky's famous observation that "beauty will save the world." For Wojtyła, this beauty is inseparable from love. For the person, who is called "to make of himself a work of art," this beauty is therefore also inseparable from freedom and conscience. Grygiel aptly concludes this chapter with a quote from Wojtyła's poem "Thinking My Country I Return to the Tree" and its defense of conscience: "History lays down events over the struggles of conscience. Victories throb inside this layer, and defeats. History does not cover them: it makes them stand out. Can history ever flow against the current of conscience?"

As Grygiel suggests in chapter 3, this defense of conscience and of the vision of the human person as a work of art inevitably leads us to the Christian vocation to holiness and to the cross. This is central to Wojtyła's understanding of the new evangelization, which requires "true witnesses of faith." In our time, this true witness is called for especially regarding the defense of marriage and family. Nazism and communism showed Wojtyła that "in marriage and the family, a decisive battle was being fought for truth and for freedom — a battle for the dignity of the human person." In chapter 4, Wojtyła's concern for married life is seen as arising out of a vision of a communion of persons in the service of a culture of love. This culture is reflected first in the relationship of the married couple to each other and in their family life and then, from there, into society at large. The reader should thus not be surprised that in chapter 5 the implications of Wojtyła's vision of the person, freedom, and communion lead us to understand that both a nation and its politics have an inherent spiritual dimension. "Every political system," Grygiel writes, "must allow itself to be 'formed by love.'" Here he makes clear that for John Paul II, the reference to the necessity of Christians working to build a "civilization of love" is not simply a pious catchphrase but a concrete proposal arising from a fundamental commandment of the Christian life — to love one's neighbor as one's self.

In these lectures, Stanisław Grygiel provides us not only with the product of a lifetime of study of the thought of Karol Wojtyła/John Paul II, but of a lifetime of experience in so many ways shaped by him. Grygiel offers us a unique vision into the life, philosophy, theology, and spirituality of one of history's great personalities and saints. It is sure to become essential reading for anyone intent on entering more fully into the conversation about and with John Paul II, or on understanding how Karol Wojtyła made of himself a work of art that astonished the world.

CARL A. ANDERSON
Supreme Knight, Knights of Columbus

Introduction

Only those who do not reflect on the human person in isolation think in conformity with the truth. An anthropology elaborated in isolation passes by the person and misses him, for the truth unveils itself only to those who live in communion with others. In its primordial form, the word about the human person cannot be reduced to opinions and hypotheses. It transcends these. A thinker whose reason constructs opinions and hypotheses relegates the primordial word about the person to the margins of his own personal life; he does not wish to receive the gift that is the truth. This kind of reason does not know the love in which and by means of which the truth reveals itself. Only those who dwell in love see the truth revealed. Reason detached from personal life cannot see this.

Words about the love that opens the human person to knowledge of the truth orient him to his source. In other words, they orient him to Love. Doubt has no power over words of love, for love never doubts. Doubt guides only those words constructed by reason. This is precisely why such words demand experimental verification if they are ever to function effectively. The person and the society subjected to doubt are thus treated as objects. They are judged not according to what (or who) they are, but according to how useful or successful they are in producing other objects, which are exchanged for ends the moment they are produced. An anthropology that is built up only with the help of such rationalistic processes is irrational — so irrational that it negates itself. In the end, *praxis*, that is, experiment, negates it. In *praxis*, it becomes evident that the human being who does not know the truth is an empty space to be filled carelessly with anything at all.

Introduction

A rational anthropology, or as Karol Wojtyła puts it, an adequate anthropology, arises in the communion of persons, since it is in this communion that the human being matures to the truth that was promised to him. An adequate anthropology is created on the basis of internal bonds that have their source in the reciprocal entrustment of persons. A person can only entrust himself to another in a certainty that excludes the need for experimental verification. Trust is not trust if one must test whether one ought to entrust oneself. Love cannot be verified in this way; we rather live from it and *become* it. A lack of faith — understood to be the reciprocal entrustment of persons — destroys both their love and their hope. Freedom is suffocated in people who do not open themselves to one another to receive the gifts of faith, hope, and love, for precisely these gifts constitute the epiphanic language of freedom. In the human person, the event of freedom takes on the colors of faith, hope, and love; it creates of him a work of art that only the words of mystics and great artists can approach.

Karol Wojtyła, who was first bishop of Krakow and then John Paul II, always remained in communion with other persons. Encounters and discussions opened him to a communal search for the "gift of God," to a communal prayer so that this gift might be realized. They opened him to a communal reception, when he and others were permitted to stand before the Transcendence of this "gift." This standing before Transcendence is the subject of Karol Wojtyła's "adequate anthropology." With his desire, the human person already dwells in the presence of the "gift of God." He exists "here," but he already lives "over there." Thanks to faith, hope, and love, man too is transcendence.

Only now do I realize that the conversations I had with Bishop Karol Wojtyła and Pope John Paul II were never an exchange about the theme, "What is man?" We spoke hypothetically about the problems tied to the institutional aspects of the Church or about the communist regime, for which the word "man" did not "loftily resound," no matter what Mr. Gorki said. But we never spoke in this way about the human person. Why? Because thanks to the freedom of faith, hope, and love, God and man formed a harmonious unity for us. We knew well that the destruction of this unity would open the way to crimes against the human person, as well as to the offense of Love with respect to God. In other words, it would open the way to sin. Bishop Karol Wojtyła and Bishop Jan Pietraszko, who spiritually influenced him, helped me to understand an intuition that had been present in me for a long while: that excessively

Introduction

distinguishing theological thought from philosophical thought, as well as from the thought proper to the exact sciences, would cause all of these — theology, philosophy, and the exact sciences — to lose their way. It would warp their *praxis*, which then devastates the human person, society, and the whole world.

Our conversations took place very spontaneously, in the least-expected moments and places. We talked without immediate or concrete goals. One could even say that we talked without any advantage. Our conversations began at the end of the 1950s, during seminars for doctoral students. These were the only conversations of ours that went in a precise direction. Since he had no other time, Bishop Wojtyła, then professor of the Catholic University at Lublin, organized these seminars for two or three days at a time in Krakow. No more than five or six people participated in each seminar. During the summer we went into the mountains, usually to Gorce, where, walking along the paths through the woods or climbing uphill, we discussed our dissertations or meditated on the classics of European philosophy, especially Aristotle's *Ethics*. We had no access to recent Western literature, for our communist "lords" hermetically isolated us from the cultural events of the West. The few books that friends brought to us from there were passed from hand to hand. We read them hastily, so that others might read them as soon as possible. But to make up for that, we could read more calmly and deeply works that had been published before the world war.

In 1962, I managed to take a nice photograph (by chance!) of our professor, as he was coming out of the woods on Mount Turbacz, which belongs to the Gorce Mountains. In this photograph, he is following a path, one of the many that inspired the title I gave to the series of books published under the aegis of the Karol Wojtyła Chair at the Pontifical John Paul II Institute for Studies on Marriage and Family in Rome: *"Sentieri della verità,"* pathways of the truth. In all the conversations I had with Bishop Wojtyła and with Pope John Paul II, a path would lead us out of the dense woods into a wide field, where the sunlight arranged nature into a harmonious ensemble of the true, the good, and the beautiful.

There were many such "pathways of the truth." We walked them at different times of the day and the night, but most often at dusk. The Cardinal was very familiar with the paths through the woods near Krakow. The so-called "sad gentlemen" (agents of the secret police) might still be seen there, but they probably wouldn't be able to overhear us. The secret police had its informers, but the Cardinal behaved clearly, transparently. He did not try to overthrow the regime imposed upon Poland.

Introduction

He limited himself to laying the spiritual foundations of a future worthy of the Polish nation. When the communist "bosses" at the time began to understand in what the work of the Archbishop of Krakow consisted, and what consequences this work might have for their rule, they began to look on him as one of the greatest enemies undermining their power. They did not know that the priest Karol Wojtyła was filled with pity for them.

John Paul II has left for the Native Land in which he was rooted, with a hope that speaks of the Promised Land. But the dead do not forsake us. They live with us, within us — they simply live in a different way. They live with us above all in the risen Christ, who is Eucharistically present on the altar. God is so faithful that he does not allow anything to take our life from us. He transfigures this life, in order to save it from annihilation. Precisely for this reason, those who still live "here" can speak to those who already live "there." Their conversation is not interrupted; it simply takes place differently.

The present volume is nothing other than a prolonged conversation with Saint John Paul II. On mountain paths or paths through the woods, we would interrupt our conversations with a silent prayer. This prayer transfigured our thinking, transforming what had begun in an exchange of words into an attentive listening to the Word that proclaimed the fulfillment of our hope. We hoped not only that our Native Land — God — would one day come to us, but that our country might regain its freedom and sovereignty. Many of us thought and said that communism would not collapse in our lifetime. Cardinal Wojtyła never said this. It is thus evident that he never even thought this. In Krakow, and even more in Rome, I was impressed by his tranquility and certainty that the "gift of God" was right next to us, and that we had only to pray and keep watch to be able to receive it at the proper time. And so it happened. Today our earthly "native land" is threatened by other dangers. Often, I think of this together with John Paul II. Our conversations continue.

One day in the spring or perhaps autumn of 1979, I found myself in John Paul II's private chapel together with André Frossard. We gazed at the kneeling Pope in silence. At one point, we glanced at each other. Later the same day, during a conference at which we both spoke, we were seated next to one another at the presider's table. Listening to the next speaker and criticizing the talk under his breath, Frossard sketched a few lines on a sheet of paper and passed it to me without saying a word. He had drawn the Pope kneeling before the altar in his chapel. In the corner

Introduction

of the drawing was a dedication that still reminds me of our gaze fixed on this white rock of prayer.

Keeping vigil over the human person, John Paul II conversed faithfully with God. He prayed even when he was not praying. Prayer shaped his thoughts and his actions. John Paul II lived on his knees before God. When he knelt in his chapel, adoring Christ in the tabernacle, I always had the impression of being in the presence of the white rock of prayer I just mentioned. I said this at the beginning of John Paul II's pontificate and I continue to repeat it, for I continue my conversations with this white rock of prayer that is now kept in my memory. We just converse differently.

The following text is an expanded version of a series of public lectures delivered from March 18 to 21, 2013, at the Pontifical John Paul II Institute for Studies on Marriage and the Family at the Catholic University of America, in Washington, D.C. The series, titled "Discovering the Human Person with John Paul II," took its place in the tradition of the McGivney Lectures, in which the Washington session of the Institute invites various theologians and philosophers of international provenance — many of them well known — to speak on themes related to the human person. The lectures are named in honor of the Venerable Father Michael J. McGivney (1852-1890), the founder of the Knights of Columbus.

Rome STANISŁAW GRYGIEL
June 29, 2013

CHAPTER 1

Vir fortis

Who was Blessed John Paul II? Only God, whose creative thought sustains every human being in existence, knows the answer to this question. None of us fully knows the being indicated by his own name. None of us knows the content of what we desire and choose about our being persons. A person's name is not a concept. It has no meaning and points to nothing except to indicate the direction in which the person exists, guided by his desire for greater goodness and beauty. According to St. Thomas Aquinas, the person's name points to the love that takes place in the space opened up within the "great question" (St. Augustine's *magna questio*), that is, the question about the mystery of the Origin and the End. We always look at the person from behind, as it were. We see his footprints on the path he has taken, leading in the direction of the Future. We see the actions with which the person enters into the laborious love of others, in order to build with them a home that belongs to all.

The human person receives his name from those who love him laboriously and to whose call he must respond just as laboriously. He receives it from those on whom he fixes his gaze. I would dare to say that this name has its origin in one person's enraptured listening to another *(ex auditu)*, or when one person fixes his gaze on the gift of love that comes to him in and through the other person.[1] When we gaze at another person, something primordial is revealed to us. Everything in our life leads back to this; everything, even the past, continues to exist in it.

1. Cf. Karol Wojtyła, "Odkupienie szuka...," in *Tutte le opere letterarie: Poesie, drammi e scritti sul teatro* (Milan: Bompiani, 2001), p. 154.

Discovering the Human Person

In the tradition of the "home" that human persons are for one another, moral obligations arise in them that are not at all to be conflated with the habits that govern present-day society. Such obligations are, rather, identical with the call with which love calls to love. Love is love insofar as it obliges us to love and, as we respond to its call, becomes ever more truly love. Moral obligations sustain in us the hope of finding in Love the salvation promised to man — the salvation we await expectantly.

The person dwells in the other person to the extent that they build a common home together. The very essence of human work consists in this being together. For this reason, to the question, "Who was John Paul II?," I would respond without hesitation: he was a person who revealed himself in the acts with which he built a "home" together with others. It is precisely in this shared building of a "home" that we must seek the answer to our question. According to Karol Wojtyła, a person reveals himself in his acts.[2] These acts show with what message the person approaches other persons — for to be a person means to be sent *(missio)*.

It is the beautiful — the "form of love"[3] — that calls man to work. The beautiful reawakens amazement and wonder in us. It fills us with eagerness for life in this world according to a logic that is not of this world. It prompts us to transform our own life into a great poetical work *(poiein)*. In doing this, the human person penetrates the meaning of his existence on this earth and understands everything with heart and mind. He becomes a friend of wisdom, a *filosofos*. The light of the beautiful allows him to look on the world and himself in a rational way. It frees his eyes, which were "hindered" (cf. Luke 24:16) because in this world, reason, closed in on itself, moves as if groping in the dark. It makes use of the cane that is its own calculation, and thus is a calculating reason *(ratio* means "calculation" and is derived from the verb *reor, reri,* to calculate).

In 1977, at the Catholic University of Milan, Cardinal Karol Wojtyła gave a conference that dealt with the sources of his vision of human life and culture. One of these sources emerges in a poem of the Polish poet Cyprian Kamil Norwid (1821-1883), "Promethidion." I think I can say that

---

2. Karol Wojtyła, *Osoba i czyn* (Krakow: Polskie Towarzystwo Teologiczne, 1969); translated by Andrzej Potocki as *The Acting Person* (Boston: D. Reidel, 1979). Cf. Stanisław Grygiel, "Czyn objawieniem osoby?," *Znak* 23, no. 2-3 = 200-201 (1971): 200-208. Cf. also Stanisław Grygiel, "Hermeneutyka czynu oraz nowy model świadomości," *Analecta Cracoviensia* 5-6 (1973-74): 139-51.

3. Cyprian Norwid, "Promethidion," in *Pisma wszystkie*, vol. 3 (Warsaw: Państwowy Instytut Wydawniczy, 1971), pp. 437, 440.

Vir fortis

in this work, Karol Wojtyła found a confirmation of his adequate anthropology.[4] Norwid writes,

> Beauty is the form of love . . .
> beauty is to make you eager to work —
> and work is for a man to gain his resurrection.[5]

Norwid's words form a keystone under which the story of man's life is composed in a harmonious ensemble. This story ends in the resurrection of the person in the other person for whom he works. The struggle with death not for the sake of honor, but for the resurrection, creates a culture of faith, hope, and love. In this struggle, the culture of the truth of man is being born.[6]

"Tell me who your friends are and I will tell you who you are," says the proverb. With whom did John Paul II build a "home"? What tradition of "work" did he help to increase as he transmitted it to others? The answers to these questions point to some extent to who he was.

John Paul II shared his life above all with laypeople. From the years of his youth to the end of his life, it was with them that he built a common home. Together with laypeople, he entered into the work of the great figures of Polish history, who have always had to struggle for freedom and learned to suffer for it. At the same time, as a priest and a bishop, he entered into the tradition of three great pastors of the Church of Krakow. On Polish soil, the history of Poland coincides with the history of the Church in the struggle for freedom — and in suffering for it.

* * *

Once, in the first years of Pope John Paul II's pontificate, I had the courage to tell him that he was very alone in the Church: "You're criticized

---

4. Karol Wojtyła, "Il problema del costituirsi della cultura attraverso la 'praxis' umana," in *Metafisica della persona: Tutte le opere filosofiche e saggi integrativi* (Milan: Bompiani, 2003), pp. 1447ff. The moral experience Wojtyła calls the *praxis* of the person is different from the *praxis* proposed by Marxism. The *praxis* of the person is an experience of love and obliges him to love, whereas Marxist *praxis* lives from struggle with the enemy. This struggle is indispensable for the survival of systems based on Marxist ideology.

5. See note 3.

6. Cf. Karol Wojtyła, "Chrześcijanin a kultura," *Znak* 16, no. 10 = 124 (1964): 1154: "'Culture' is one of those terms intimately bound to man, which define his earthly existence and in a certain way denote his very existence."

not only by theologians, but by priests and even bishops. Holy Father, they don't understand you!" After reflecting for a while, he answered, "I am not alone. The laity are with me." In John Paul II's consciousness, a priestly life shared with laypeople confirmed the evangelical truth of Norwid's words: "Man? . . . *he is a high priest unaware,/And unformed.*"[7]

From his high school years in Wadowice to the years of the Petrine ministry, John Paul II asked the question about man in a poetical-philosophical and poetical-priestly way. He asked this question in dialogue with others and again in the Eucharistic offering (in his priestly life there was not a single day that lacked this *introibo* to the altar of the Lord). Kneeling before the God-man, John Paul II knelt together with him before the human person to wash his tired feet. He knelt before God, who burns with love for man; and before man, who burns for God. He never knelt before circumstances.

On March 8, 1964, as he was installed as Archbishop of Krakow in Wawel Cathedral, he said, "I think that to be a pastor means to know how to receive everything that others contribute and the burdens that others carry." To know how to receive means, to a large extent, to know how to give. It is to know how to coordinate, to put together, so that out of all this, the good that is common to all can grow — so that each of us has his or her place in the work of salvation, in the divine plan. Each of us is a great treasure.[8]

As he matured in his humanity and in his priesthood, Karol Wojtyła saw ever more clearly that he was sent to all. His priestly experience of man gave him the words that we find in the 1986 Letter to Priests: "The priest . . . is ordained . . . to bring people into the new life made accessible by Christ . . . to gather them into his body. . . . In a word, our identity as priests is manifested in the 'creative' exercise of the love for souls communicated by Christ Jesus."[9] At the funeral of another priest, he said that priests fight "for the same cause for which

---

7. Cyprian Norwid, "The Sphinx," in *Poems*, trans. Danuta Borchardt (Brooklyn, NY: Archipelago Books, 2011), p. 33; originally published as "Sfinks (II)," in *Pisma wszystkie*, vol. 2 (Warsaw: Państwowy Instytut Wydawnicz, 1971), p. 33.

8. Cf. Adam Boniecki, *Kalendarium życia Karola Wojtyły* (Krakow: Znak, 1979), p. 216.

9. John Paul II, "Letter of the Holy Father Pope John Paul II to All the Priests of the Church on the Occasion of Holy Thursday 1986," no. 10 in *Letters to My Brother Priests: Complete Collection of Holy Thursday Letters (1979-2005)*, 5th ed. (Woodbridge, IL: Midwest Theological Forum, 2006), p. 121.

Christ fought, and for which the Church fights . . . for the most basic right of man: to know God."[10]

As Archbishop of Krakow, Karol Wojtyła continued to open the doors of his house to all people at all times — even at night, if necessary. One could enter directly from the street. He was awake. He was not afraid to receive people even when meeting them could pose a great risk to himself. In the 1970s, I twice accompanied a Russian professor of the Soviet Academy of Sciences to the Archbishop's residence. The man's father had been a general and hero of the Soviet Union, who had worked closely with the notorious Lavrentiy Beria, Marshal of the Soviet Union and chief of the Ministry of State Security (NKVD), or the secret police. These dangerous nighttime conversations bore much fruit for the universal Church. They ended with a blessing imparted by Cardinal Wojtyła to the kneeling Russian, whose baptism had been kept secret even from his mother (his father was already dead). When his mother learned of it, she suffered a heart attack. In those same years, I brought to the Cardinal by night two Russian women of Jewish origin, professors at the University of Moscow, who subsequently were baptized in Warsaw. The courage of Karol Wojtyła had its source in his complete entrustment of himself to the truth and its consequences.

I always had the impression that John Paul II felt more at ease in the company of laypeople than of clerics. The first layperson to form Wojtyła's relation with God was his father. Through prayer, his father's love — which was also full of maternal care for the boy who had lost his mother — opened the child's filial love to the Love that unites the Father with the Son in the Holy Trinity. Together with his father, the young Karol began to participate in the Spirit of Love who unites Father and Son in the triune life of God.[11] It may be that already then, God began to open the young boy of Wadowice to bearing the responsibility contained in the words, "It has seemed good to the Holy Spirit and to us" (Acts 15:28). I say this with trepidation, because I know that I am touching the mystery of John Paul II's person. The mystery that each person is cannot be the object of opinions and experimental verification. Words that point to the

---

10. Karol Wojtyła, homily on the occasion of the funeral Mass for Fr. Stanisław Bajer, May 7, 1963. Cited in Tomasz Bajer and Katarzyna Dybeł, *"Dobrze używałeś kapłaństwa, mój bracie . . .": Księża Stanisław i Andrzej Bajerowie; świadectwo życia, świadectwo epoki* (Krakow: Wydawnictwo "Czuwajmy," 2011), p. 184.

11. Cf. John Paul II, *Crossing the Threshold of Hope*, trans. Jenny McPhee and Martha McPhee (New York: Knopf, 1994), pp. 128-29.

mystery of a person's spiritual life must be pronounced with deep reverence — and not before we have removed the sandals from our feet to avoid trampling anything.

Great things must have been awakened in the young Wojtyła as he listened attentively to the words of the tailor Jan Tyranowski and perceived the fire in them. Wojtyła the mature priest wrote an article bearing witness to Jan's person. The words of this text point far beyond their immediate meaning and describe not only the tailor, but also the student who listened to him.[12] Jan Tyranowski's learning did not reach the heights of the young Wojtyła's, and yet it was not Wojtyła who was the teacher. Above all, Jan understood what man cannot learn from books but can only receive from God. He was a burning bush afire with God. He gazed at God and God gazed at him. Jan's *facere*, his "doing," was very small, but his *esse*, his "being," was great. From it flowed his great *agere*, that is, his great love and profound understanding of the human person. This tailor who lived on the outskirts of Krakow educated young men without having the faintest idea of education. He simply gave them what he himself became while seeking God. He spoke to them of his life with God and in God. According to Wojtyła, Jan spoke very imperfectly, and yet his words were more adequate to the mysteries of man and of God than many academic ruminations. So it is not surprising if Jan influenced Wojtyła's way of thinking and philosophizing. The person and acts of Jan Tyranowski were the source of the first, unconscious inspiration of *Person and Act*. Meditating on the human person and God with the tailor, Karol Wojtyła saw how the human person is an event of divine and human love and of divine and human truth. It is precisely this event that we see from a distance, never directly.

Karol Wojtyła learned from Jan in particular moments, for example, the night when Wojtyła and other young men listened into the morning hours as the tailor spoke of the human being's intimacy with God. That night, the student Wojtyła listened to the "voices" that reached him through phrases that may have been unsophisticated or grammatically incorrect, but in which Jan Tyranowski opened and gave himself. Listening attentively to Jan's words about shared life with God, Wojtyła saw that the human person is great when he is an epiphany of God.

The tailor Tyranowski introduced the young Wojtyła to the world of mysticism at a time when the Nazi lie raged over Europe with calculated

---

12. Karol Wojtyła, "Apostoł," *Tygodnik Powszechny*, no. 35 (1949).

precision and the Russian lash had already begun to strike Poland. In the young men who listened to him, Tyranowski laid the mystical foundations of the house of freedom. With the help of great mystics such as St. John of the Cross and St. Louis Grignon de Montfort, he taught them to win their freedom through a daily labor that did not mark the price. Within the space of the experience of their persons, in communion with other persons and without textbooks, he taught them to read the Bible, poetry, and the works of great thinkers. He went ahead of them, opening himself to the person of Christ. In Christ, they found the "living water" (John 4:10) that quenched their desire for the reality that is the farthest away and at the same time the closest to man.

By being present to him, Jan Tyranowski showed Wojtyła what it means to be present to man. Karol Wojtyła profited from this dialogue of gifts that took place in the tailor's tiny room — as a priest, a bishop, and finally as pope. From Fr. Wojtyła's experience as pastor of the students and professors of Krakow, the group was born that called itself the *Środowisko*, or, roughly translated, "milieu." Many of these young people who prayed together and shared vacations with him matured in a holiness, the visible sign of which is now the Servant of God Jerzy Ciesielski. Ciesielski was a professor at the Polytechnic University of Krakow who died with two of his children in a tragic accident on the Nile in 1970.[13]

Preparing these young people for marriage, Wojtyła the priest "learned to love human love." He learned to understand better the sacramental mystery of marriage. He had not been called to this state of life, but participated in it through the conjugal love of the persons entrusted to him. This is the genesis of the book *Love and Responsibility*. The conversations he had with Jerzy Ciesielski accompanied Archbishop Wojtyła in his work on Vatican Council II's Dogmatic Constitution on the Church in the Modern World, *Gaudium et Spes*.

The group of actors that formed around the person of Mieczysław Kotlarczyk, the founder of the Rhapsodic Theater, provided an analogous environment. In this form of drama, the word itself played the fundamental role: the beautiful word reveals the ethical and moral force of a human love that is tied to the truth.[14] Wojtyła was an actor in this

---

13. Karol Wojtyła, "Wspomnienie o Jerzym Ciesielskim," *Tygodnik Powszechny*, no. 51-52 (1970); translated as "Remembering Jerzy Ciesielski," *Communio: International Catholic Review* 29, no. 4 (Winter 2002): 746-51.

14. Karol Wojtyła, "Sul teatro della parola," in *Tutte le opere letterarie*, pp. 967ff.

Theater, which staged clandestine performances in private apartments during the war — an activity for which the participants could have been arrested or deported to a concentration camp. After the war, the Communists tolerated this theater only up to a point. They did not have the courage to shut it down entirely. Once he had returned from his studies in the West, Wojtyła participated in the life of the Theater, but only externally. In it, he learned how to transmit the word, in its material and content, to others. Everyone received the fruits of his work in the Theater when he transmitted to us not only the words of poets, but the Word of the Living God. A man must be present in the word he speaks to others. Only someone who speaks to others in such a way that he offers himself, knows how much work is required to transmit the Word with which God reveals both himself and man. This means that in giving to man what man is, God also gives himself. God desires that in his Word, the human word should also be present.

The theater clarified something essential for Wojtyła: in order to speak the word of the poet well and truly, first one must entrust oneself to his person. The poet's person is his first word. All his other words come afterward. It is impossible to entrust oneself to them if one has not entrusted oneself to the Word that is their creator. The theater is a school of theology: God is Word. The Word is reflected in such a mysterious way in the words of the gospel that we will contemplate these words in an endless wonder.

This experience of the Rhapsodic Theater in a time so hostile to man, revealed to Wojtyła that building up the house of freedom cannot be a solitary enterprise. Freedom is always the freedom of the communion of persons. For this reason, every form of totalitarianism will always wage war against interpersonal relations. It will destroy them with force and terror, because the truth that makes us free is revealed precisely in these relationships. Where friendship, marriage, and the family are affronted, then without a doubt we are dealing with a totalitarian system of one kind or another. At the threshold of family homes, totalitarian systems lose their power; they are overcome by a mysticism of love. The memory of even a single love not lived *ad experimentum* will ceaselessly point people to the path to be taken, even if in public life they can find no indicators of it.

Freedom demands the moral rectitude of persons, which is a fruit of love. The human person becomes morally upright in friendship, in marriage, in the family, in the nation, that is, *in ecclesia*, in the Church. In these personal communions, people confess and give themselves to one another. And only these upright human beings know what lies and moral iniquity are. So we should not be surprised if, in times when freedom is despised, the secret police surround with particular "care" those who dare to enter the tradition of a courageous and laborious being-together-with-others, a reciprocal entrustment, a faith in the fruits of a shared search for the truth in love. The priest Fr. Karol Wojtyła was one of the strongest links of this tradition.

The tradition of courageous love, that is, the tradition of responding with love to the Love that created the human person, gave rise in Wojtyła to an anthropology that was adequate to the divine-human truth. This truth calls us to journey toward it. Karol Wojtyła perceived this divine-human truth in the human person's moral experience. Within the tradition of the laborious being-together-with-others, he matured in the Tradition of the laborious being-together-with-God. In God, together with others, he built up the *communio personarum*. The word *communio* is derived from the words *munus* (task) and *cum* (with): *cum munere* means to live with a task. Every person is a task, a *munus*, for other persons. His presence obliges other persons to be present in the same way for him. Each person bears personal obligations *(munia sustinet)*. These obligations defend freedom by binding human love to the truth to which it belongs. Obligations form a defensive bastion for freedom, both discovered and built up in moral experience. The person is tasked with it *(munita, from munio, -ire)*. The person must give thanks to other persons for this fortification.

The person helps other persons to bear burdens; he calls them to solidarity, to which he himself is also called. Persons belong reciprocally to one another. This is the content of the word *"solidarność"* [solidarity]. Wojtyła focused his attention on this category in *Person and Act*, ten years before the Polish Solidarity movement saw the light of day. He discovered this path to freedom in the moral experience in which his philosophical thought had its beginnings. In moral experience, the human person attains himself. He becomes conscious, that is, present to reality.[15] He enters into solidarity with it.

John Paul II's pastoral work consisted in a shared, laborious seeking with others — seeking that reality to which we all belong. But it is as if we

---

15. It is worth noting that in German, "presence to reality" or attention is indicated by the word *Geistesgegenwart*, literally, the presence of the spirit.

have lost it somewhere at the beginning of the path, so it is not easy for us to ask questions about it.

> I will say of work — that it is seeking what we lost,
> hence the song — a continual recalling.[16]

Wojtyła found "what we lost" in the person of Christ. Charged *(munitus)* with this greatest Task *(munus)*, which he continually rediscovered and renewed in his interior and in the interior of others, he proceeded with imperturbable serenity toward the Future with those who were entrusted to him, through the night of contempt for man.

The human person remembers the Future insofar as he remembers the Past. "What we lost" is simultaneously our Past and our Future. We bear it in our interior, and it is there that we must seek it. In seeking it, man matures into himself.

> Maturity: a descent to a hidden core,
> . . . .
> the soul more reconciled with the body,
> but more opposed to death,
> uneasy about the resurrection.
> Maturing toward difficult encounters.
>
> Maturity is also fear;
> the end of cultivation is already its beginning,
> the beginning of wisdom is fear,
> based on a different layer of the same soil.[17]

The pastoral work of the priest Karol Wojtyła had the character of poetry. It sang of what was "lost" and sought in the human person. For this reason, it did not fall into the routine that entraps those who produce pastoral "objects" almost as if to profit by them. We cannot approach the person with our own industry. We journey toward him, following the traces he has left behind in words that are acts and in acts that are words.

---

16. Cyprian Norwid, "Promethidion — Bogumił," in *Pisma wszystkie*, vol. 3, p. 439.
17. Karol Wojtyła, "Meditations on Death: Thoughts on Maturing," in *The Place Within: The Poetry of Pope John Paul II*, trans. Jerzy Peterkiewicz (New York: Random House, 1994), p. 153.

Vir fortis

God leaves similar traces in his creature *(vestigia Dei)*. In following them, we call his Person and await his response. When a person passes by, having drawn near to us, the beauty that remains in us as a trace reawakens wonder in us. We can do justice to this beauty only through reflection and contemplative silence. This is how we do justice to man and to God, who

> ... is there. Only a tremor here,
> only words retrieved from nothingness.
> Oh — and a particle still remains
> of that amazement which will become the essence
> of eternity.[18]

As Wojtyła says, this is the love without which man cannot live.[19]

> Love explained all for me,
> all was resolved by love,
> so this love I adore
> wherever it may be.[20]

The human person prays with the silence that expresses this love. With this word, Wojtyła drew near not only to God, but also to man. Prayer gave form to his life and to his person from the first years of his youth, just as it had given form to the life and person of his father in Wadowice. The father's prayer impressed itself deeply into the heart and the memory of the son. Every time I entered John Paul II's private chapel in the Vatican for Holy Mass, the first thing that struck me was a white rock of prayer leaning there on the prie-dieu. He was in conversation with God even when he was not speaking with him. Every time Bishop Wojtyła and I found ourselves in a car together, our conversations were only suspensions of silence, crumbs of his prayer. Prayer framed our conversations during the walks we took — outside of the city to avoid the police eavesdropping via wiretaps.

I am convinced that conversation with God was for him a school for conversation with human beings. When he spoke with someone, he looked at the other person and listened to him attentively, as if entrusting himself

---

18. Karol Wojtyła, "Song of the Hidden God: Shores of Silence," in *Place Within*, p. 4.
19. Cf. John Paul II, *Redemptor hominis*, encyclical letter, March 4, 1979, no. 10.
20. Wojtyła, "Song of the Hidden God: Shores of Silence," p. 6.

to the other's words and person, just as he entrusted himself to God and his Word. He listened more than he spoke. And when he spoke, he did not get entangled in the problem at hand, but spoke to the human being present in it, to whom he entrusted himself. He simply looked at the interlocutors who hid themselves from him. There was no reproach in his eyes. There was only sorrow because, as he said, "we don't understand each other." One day, after having listened to a fairly well-known Italian priest give an aggressive reply in defense of his own actions, John Paul II simply said, "I see that now nothing is left to me but to go into the chapel and pray!" There, from this white rock of prayer, God doubtless drew the word that, after a little while, that priest heard echoing within him.

If only God knows what is in man, then only in prayer can the truth of man be known. The pastor who prays little or not at all is not a pastor, because he does not know man. If he does not speak to God, he will not know how to speak to human beings to help them know themselves and God. To seek "what we lost" means to seek the plan that God determined in his Son for all eternity for each person, in the act of creation. Karol Wojtyła, priest, bishop, and finally pope, focused his and our attention on the Person of Christ, "the center of the universe and history."[21] He taught us to stand at the foot of the cross and to gaze rationally at the empty tomb, to seek there the first Love, that is, the act of creation that is ever new. He helped others to be reborn and vice versa. The human person knows himself when he converts to others and is reborn in them.

The mystery is dazzlingly bright. It is impossible to gaze directly at it. We can merely look upon the visible world rationally in its invisible light. The human person is a mystery like the Mystery of God. Wojtyła's adequate anthropology is indebted to the light of both these mysteries. The light of the Word-Act of the living God revealed to Karol Wojtyła the truth about man, as indicated by the word-acts of his person. At the same time, the light that radiates from the word-acts of the human person allowed him to enter more deeply into the Word-Act God addresses to man. Karol Wojtyła came to know man by praying to God, and he came to know God by dialoguing with man in the attitude of prayer. Anyone who tries to know God and man in any other way will know neither. He will know only his own thoughts.

The experience of prayer as pastoral work gave Wojtyła ample evidence that without prayer, theology dies and anthropology is anything

---

21. John Paul II, *Redemptor hominis*, 1.

Vir fortis

but anthropology. The Word of God present in the faith called *fides quae* forms a unity with the anthropology that seeks to comprehend man in his act of faith, called *fides qua*. The philosopher lives in passage, in the Pasch; he dies in the act *fides qua*, in the hope of rising in the Word that is already present in the *fides quae*. Anthropology has meaning to the extent that it stretches upward toward the Word that is not man's own word. It has meaning to the extent that it stretches upward toward the mouth of the living God, *ad ora Dei viventis*, which speaks this Word. Listening to the Word who is Christ, man adores, *adora*, God who generates and reveals the Word. The adoration of the Word who is the Son of God renders justice to his Father and also to man. I think that Wojtyła's adequate anthropology that stretches upward *ad ora*, to the mouth of the living God, crystallized in all those who gazed at this white rock of prayer leaning there on the kneeler. The adequate answer to the question "Who is man?" reaches us in the silence in which we adore God present in man.[22]

Dialoguing with God and with men, Karol Wojtyła was silent and listened more than he spoke. His gaze told his interlocutor what he thought of what he had heard from him. To artists, who should know how to listen to silence and through it, to speak, he recalled the words, *"In patientia vestra possidebitis animas vestras"* [In patience you will possess your souls] (Luke 21:19).[23] He taught them to wait patiently for others and to seek them with the same patience. In revealing themselves to others, they would bear witness to man's truth with words full of silence. Silence is truth's weapon, the weapon of love for man.

This patience and silence revealed the greatness of the hope that Karol Wojtyła placed in God. He once showed me a letter in which a well-known European theologian asked him to modify the Church's conjugal ethics. The theologian argued for his own position by citing the fact that people had abandoned and were continuing to abandon the Church because of the Pope's inflexible teaching. He asked me, "What do you think?" From "behind clenched teeth," as Homer says (*The Odyssey*, XIX), the words escaped me: "But this is stupid! He forgot that Christ was al-

---

22. It is worthwhile recalling the words of St. Thomas Aquinas here: "Actus autem credentis non terminatur ad enuntiabile sed ad rem" (*Summa theologiae*, II-II, q. 1, a. 2, ad 2).

23. Cf. Karol Wojtyła, *Ewangelia a sztuka: Rekolekcje dla artystów* (Krakow: Instytut Dialogu Międzykulturowego im. Jana Pawła II, 2011), p. 66. This text was originally given by Wojtyła as a retreat, April 16-18, 1962.

ready in a situation like this centuries ago, and asked the twelve who remained with him, 'Do you also wish to go away?'" (John 6:67). After a moment of silence, the Pope said simply, "Yes, that's true, but who will tell him this?" And he withdrew to his chapel to pray.

John Paul II listened attentively to the human person's first word, which is his body oriented to the other person. The interior life of the human person expresses itself first of all in the body. It expresses itself in the unity of man and woman. Together with the faithful, in the course of his first papal catecheses, John Paul II listened to this word that is the human body. In a reflection full of wonder, he contemplated its beauty, which unites man and woman in one flesh. Those who do not contemplate man and woman who are "one flesh," think of their bodies as they think of the abstract products of reason. They do not entrust themselves to its beauty, because they do not know to love it. They turn it into the object of their manipulation. It is their "sarcophobia,"[24] or fear of the body, that devastates our society today.

* * *

Man is like a tree. He grows from earth cultivated by those who have already disappeared, and enters into their work. He is rooted in the Past and the Future, that is, in the Love that creates and saves man. With hope, he responds to the voice of the Promise that reaches him from beyond history. "The *past* is *today*, only a little further," Norwid writes.[25] Similarly, the future is today, only a little further ahead of us. In the past and the future we find the house of our fathers, our country.

> When I think my Country —
> I express what I am, anchoring my roots.
> And this is what the heart tells,
> as if a hidden frontier ran from me to others,
> embracing us all within a past
> older than each of us;
> and from this past I emerge
> when I think my Country,
> I take her into me as a treasure,

---

24. From the Greek *sarx*, which means body.
25. Cyprian Norwid, "II Przeszłość," in *Pisma wszystkie*, vol. 2, p. 18.

constantly wondering how to increase it,
how to give a wider measure to that space
it fills withal.²⁶

To ask about and to seek one's country, that is, to ask about and to seek the meaning of life, were part of Karol Wojtyła's questions about the truth of the human person. In everything that happened in his life, which he united with the lives of others, they were part of his seeking.

The three great bishops of Krakow, along with two great religious of the same diocese, had a great influence on Karol Wojtyła's priestly and episcopal service. Their spiritual presence helped him to give a beautiful form to his life and work. They taught him how to be prudently courageous, so that his service could help people in their work to "gain their resurrection."

The first of these was the martyr-bishop St. Stanislas, in whom Polish bishops find the model for their pastoral work. He ceaselessly reminds them that they bear responsibility for a people, and that they must oppose themselves absolutely to every authority that injures this people.

St. Stanislas lived from 1030 to circa 1079, and became bishop of Krakow in 1072. In 1079, when he did not hesitate to tell King Boleslas the Bold, "You may not behave in this way!" and excommunicated him, the king had him murdered before the altar. Cardinal Wojtyła dedicated his penultimate poem, "Stanislas," written in 1978, to his holy predecessor:

> There was a man; through him my land saw
> it was bound to heaven.
> There was such a man, there were such people, such always are —
> Through them the earth sees itself in the sacrament
> of a new existence. It is a fatherland,
> for here the Father's house is begotten and here is born.
> I want to describe my Church in the man whose name was Stanislas.
> And King Boleslas wrote this name with his sword
> in the ancient chronicles,
> wrote this name with his sword on the cathedral's marble floor
> as the streams of blood were flowing
> over the marble floor.²⁷

26. Karol Wojtyła, "Thinking My Country," in *Place Within*, p. 141.
27. Karol Wojtyła, "Stanislas," in *Place Within*, pp. 179-80.

The direct predecessor of Metropolitan Archbishop Wojtyła in the episcopal seat of Krakow was Cardinal Prince Adam Sapieha (1867-1951), who became bishop of Krakow in 1911.[28] Sapieha, called "the unbreakable prince," was national hero, protector of the poor, and defender of the persecuted and victims of the oppressive regimes. Risking prison and his own life, he cried out to the German occupiers and then to the Communist authorities, "You may not behave in this way!" Both the Nazis and the Communists respected him; they were downright afraid of him. The Communists began a trial to convict him only after his death.

Bishop Wojtyła entered the Cathedral of Krakow to be installed as Metropolitan Archbishop with a certain reverent fear. "When today I found myself before the tomb of St. Stanislas, I realized that in front of this altar lies my . . . I am afraid to say it . . . my predecessor. I am afraid to say it because everyone in Poland knows what this name means . . . Adam Stefan Cardinal Sapieha." Wojtyła could not stop marveling that he was Sapieha's successor. Astonished at the nomination, he confided to Monsignor Stanisław Czartoryski, "I, successor to Cardinal Sapieha?" In the square outside the Archbishop's residence in Krakow, he had a statue of Sapieha erected without asking permission of the government authorities; he simply told them what he was planning to do. On June 16, 1999, looking out from the window of the Archbishop's residence at that square, John Paul II said, "Here is the statue of the Cardinal . . . the Unbreakable Prince. . . . Father Cardinal, for what you were for us, for me, for all Poles during the time of the terrible occupation, I say to you: May God reward you!"

From the experience of history, Cardinal Karol Wojtyła and then John Paul II learned that when man entrusts himself to the consequences of the truth, he becomes unbreakable. The nation is unbreakable that has people who wait with courage for the victory of truth. The truth does not need to be defended. "Truth can never be refuted!" says Socrates to Polos.[29] Those who do not resist with it are already conquered. "Weak is a people that accepts defeat, forgetting that it was sent to keep watch till the

---

28. Eugeniusz Baziak, the Archbishop of Lviv who was expelled from his see by the Russians immediately after World War II, was named Archbishop of Krakow in 1963, after twelve years in which the see was empty after Sapieha's death. Baziak died before announcing his nomination to the Metropolitan Chapter of Krakow. Thus, according to canon law, Karol Wojtyła was the direct successor of Sapieha.

29. Plato, *Gorgias* 473b. All translations of Plato are taken from Plato, *Complete Works*, ed. John M. Cooper (Indianapolis: Hackett, 1997).

Vir fortis

coming of its hour. And the hours keep returning on the great clockface of history."[30] A people is weak when its members are so weak that they are no longer present to one another because of a lack of reciprocal trust. Then the truth remains hidden and forgotten; it ceases to be that which the Greeks called *alethia*, that is, "not-forgetting." Then people live in the lie and nourish themselves on it.

The coincidence of two facts seems more and more important to me. The pact entered into by Primate Stefan Wyszyński and the Polish bishops, which introduced the *modus vivendi* between the Catholic Church in Poland and the Communist government, does not bear the signature of Cardinal Sapieha. One of the articles of this pact obliged ordinaries to promise loyalty with respect to the government. During a conversation, John Paul II said to me, "You know, I am the only bishop that did not make this promise of loyalty." "How did that happen?" I asked. "I don't know," he replied. "I simply didn't go to their office and 'they' didn't insist." During the German occupation, the seminarian Wojtyła had lived in the house of the Unbreakable Prince, Sapieha, with a few companions, studying philosophy and theology. The experience left an indelible mark on all of them. In difficult and dangerous times, Sapieha's unbreakability showed them the way and gave them heart.

After St. Stanislas and Cardinal Sapieha, the third bishop who influenced the form of Karol Wojtyła's pastoral service was the Servant of God bishop Jan Pietraszko. Pietraszko was the older of the two by a few years, but Wojtyła chose him as his own auxiliary bishop. Bishop Pietraszko opened to Wojtyła the path to youth, as John Paul II himself testified in a telegram to Krakow on the occasion of Pietraszko's death. Jan Pietraszko was still a young priest in the years immediately following the Second World War. Left behind by Sapieha, whose secretary he was twice, he began to organize the pastoral care of university students in Krakow. Each of his homilies stirred the city's professors and students; as soon as they were printed, they sold out and were passed from hand to hand. The bishop wrote out all of his homilies. He was unable to speak without having prepared beforehand. During the funeral Mass celebrated for him in St. Anne's Church, where he had remained pastor even after his episcopal ordination, an unfinished homily was read, which had been found in his typewriter. He had been preparing it for

---

30. Karol Wojtyła, "Thinking My Country: Thinking My Country I Return to the Tree," in *Place Within*, p. 149.

the following Sunday. It was a reflection on suffering and death — almost his testament.

For me, Bishop Jan is one of the Fathers of the Church. My wife and I were witnesses when, one evening, Pope John Paul II said to him, "Bishop Jan, I learn theology from you!" And not only theology. Just as he was for us laypeople, Bishop Jan Pietraszko was for Father and Bishop Wojtyła, and for John Paul II, a great witness to God's presence for and in man.

Bishop Jan Pietraszko told me of his first meeting with Karol Wojtyła. It took place during the war in the apartment of Archbishop Sapieha, whose secretary Pietraszko was at the time. One evening the Archbishop told him that the following morning, a young student, a worker, would come to serve Mass: "Father, give him a good breakfast; he needs it! He has a great future before him, take care of him!" The next day, early in the morning, a thin young man arrived holding an armful of books tied together with string. It was Karol Wojtyła.

God writes our earthly history in heaven in a marvelous way. During the obscure night of the occupation, two men met who would draw out of themselves so much light for the Church and for Poland. At that moment, no one would have stumbled upon the thought that this poor worker-student would one day appoint as his auxiliary bishop the priest who had once served him breakfast in Sapieha's residence. Great men seek out and encounter great men; with their help, they become great. Only great men feel in the presence of other great men that which I call *timor hominis*, the reverent "fear of men," like the *timor Dei*, the fear of God. John Paul II once said to me that when he addressed priests or laypeople in the presence of Bishop Jan, he watched the latter's face constantly. "If he wrinkled his brow or gave me a look, these were signs to me that I had said something I shouldn't have said."

Their thoughts and acts were in consonant harmony, and adapted themselves not only to the circumstances but to the truth to be sought. They helped us to live in the darkness of communism, which seemed as if it would cover us our whole lives. In the presence of these priests, we could catch sight of the dawn. A communion of persons arose around them that radiated the Church and freedom.

Every day, these two men waited for people in the confessional and before the altar — the last bastions of freedom. They served with Christ's forgiveness, and with his presence in the Eucharist. Both could not endure pastoral bureaucracy. Like the Good Samaritan in the Gospel, they cared for the wounds that evil had inflicted on human beings. They did all in their power so that others might have a better life.[31]

As university chaplains, they taught us to look at life in the light of the Bible and to read the Bible in the light of daily life. This allowed us to judge not only our lives, but the political situation from which, humanly speaking, we saw no escape. Without entering into active political opposition, they transmitted to us the immutable foundations of acting for the common good — the good that is the person of every human being. They taught us to engage in true politics, in the deepest meaning of the term. The latter hinges on the capacity to see and to read the "signs of the times," and to find in them the truth entrusted to our work for the good of every human being.

Neither Wojtyła nor Pietraszko needed methods learned from a pastoral handbook. The two men never spoke of such things. Their pastoral work consisted simply in their presence before God in everything they thought and did. Present to God, they were also present to the people in church, in their homes, and in the street. As chaplains, they prayed with people, visited them and vacationed with them. They did not impose on anyone. They were characterized by a certain shyness, which was more visible in Bishop Jan than in Cardinal Wojtyła. The latter surprised me once by confiding to me how much effort it cost him at the beginning of his episcopal ministry to face the challenge of encountering the people of the universities of Krakow — and not only them. Both men radiated a strength, especially at the altar and the pulpit, and in the confessional — the strength of the Eucharistic priesthood, with which their persons were identified.

A final great influence on the formation of John Paul II's person were two insurgents of the January Uprising of 1863. These men fought against the Russians for the freedom of Poland, which three invaders, Russia, Prussia, and Austria, erased from the political map of Europe for almost 150 years. From such patriots, Wojtyła learned the love that defends man when he is threatened in his being — by the aggressor as well as by material and cultural poverty.[32] It was granted to him to elevate both of them to the honors of the altar, as St. Albert Chmielowski, painter and founder

---

31. Karol Wojtyła and Jerzy Ciesielski wrote about this in "List do redakcji w sprawie campingu," *Homo Dei* 3, no. 81 (May-June 1957): 420-23. Cf. also Wanda Półtawska, *Beskidzkie rekolekcje: Dzieje przyjaźni księdza Karola Wojtyły z rodziną Połtawskich* (Częstochowa: Święty Paweł, 2009).

32. Karol Wojtyła, *I miei amici* (Bologna: CSEO, 1980).

of a religious order in Krakow that cared for the poor and abandoned, and St. Rafał Kalinowski, a Carmelite priest.

John Paul II had to meet these two men in a purely spiritual way, but the chronological distance between them did not weaken the ties that bound them. In articles dedicated to these figures, Bishop Wojtyła narrated how communion of life with them transformed his person. Both patriots imbued him with the light of the mystery of heroism, which consists in facing death in defense of the "shared task" (Norwid) that is one's country.[33]

Rafał Kalinowski had been condemned to death as a Minister of War of the Polish insurrection, but his sentence was commuted to a deportation to Siberia. Returning over a decade later, he entered Carmel. Brother Albert, when still very young, lost a leg during the January Uprising. He became a well-known painter, and was secretly in love with a great actress of international renown, Helena Modrzejewska. But in the end he abandoned everything to offer his life to the outcasts of society. Every year, on Christmas Eve, Bishop Wojtyła shared the traditional Christmas wafer *(opłatek)* with these poor, in the shelter founded by Brother Albert in Krakow.

* * *

What did I receive from Blessed John Paul II? This is a difficult question for me to answer. He directed my doctoral thesis, but he was not an academic professor to me. He did not hold erudition to be very important. Instead, he was interested in a student's thought — the thought that arose from the person's experience and that strove to encompass and express it. Our conversations contained more silence than words, more indicating the Invisible than defining the things we can see and grasp. Along with Bishop Jan Pietraszko, he taught me to look in the direction from which come the "voices" that beckon us to interpret them — and to change our life. Rilke affirms that only the saints know how to listen to these "voices" of the Invisible.[34] Wojtyła and Pietraszko knew how to listen to them. At the time I was not mature enough to be able to listen on my knees with these men to the news about the human person that

---

33. Karol Wojtyła, "Dwaj powstańcy," *Tygodnik Powszechny*, no. 35 (1963).

34. Cf. Rainer Maria Rilke, "The First Elegy," in *Duino Elegies: A Bilingual Edition*, trans. Stephen Cohn (Evanston, IL: Northwestern University Press, 1998), pp. 21-25.

reached me from "over there." But in their presence, I sensed that man is only comprehensible from "there." "Here," this comprehensibility begins to be revealed only in the light emanating from holy men and women.

Professor Wojtyła was an autodidact. Perhaps for this reason, he did not hinder us, his students, from seeking the truth with our own strength. He did not demand erudition; rather, he simply led us to the source. Kneeling together with us there, he contemplated the pure water that flowed from it. With it, we together quenched our thirst. Reawakening in his students an enthusiasm for the truth, he introduced them to life in God, *en theo* (this is precisely the etymological meaning of the word "enthusiasm"). A wonder-filled enthusiasm at that which both begins and seeks its fulfillment in love protected the students from both relativism and the fundamentalism with which Marxism poisoned the life of society. The truth embraces and penetrates us in changing circumstances, always pointing us in the unchanging direction we must travel to seek it. Each of us searches for it in the way proper to his being a person. Professor Wojtyła did not forget that every human being simultaneously marvels and trembles before that which comes *(advenire)*, or that God carries on a unique and unrepeatable dialogue with every human being. People's otherness did not distance Wojtyła from them; it united him with them. In personal otherness was born that unique and unrepeatable *universitas magistri et studentium* between Professor Wojtyła and each student, built upon the truth sought in love.

Fidelity to the original experience of man and of the world allowed Karol Wojtyła to think originally *(origo* means source, beginning). He did not repeat the arguments of other authors. The erudite lost their heads in his presence. Their knowledge, borrowed from others, hindered them from concentrating on the original moments of the person's experience, on the true and on the good — the search for which is vain if it is reduced to argumentation. Wojtyła did not allow himself to fall under the spell of the drawing room-style fashion of discussing the most recent products of calculating reason *(ratio)*. Thinking in a vacuum was something alien to him; it lacked the support of an intellectual vision and a similarly intellectual reading *(intellectus)* of reality.

Karol Wojtyła inspired in his students an atmosphere of happiness — the happiness without which one cannot think logically. The gift of happiness comes to us through the presence of others received in our own conscience; it is in our conscience that we welcome this gift. Happiness comes as the fruit of acts in which the person fulfills himself in the love of truth, which represents the eternal Future that reveals itself to him in other persons. It is this eternal Future that gives man his dignity. Justifying the lie through argumentation makes people unhappy, because it deprives them of the Future. When the lie crushes them because of their fidelity to the truth, the gift of beatitude awaits them in the depths of their suffering.

Karol Wojtyła's thought was mystically existential. He was not Hegel's owl, which flies by night to see what happened during the day.[35] Wojtyła's thought was the contemporary of events in which, "here and now," he matured toward a Future. This Future is so transcendent with respect to human acts and thought that it caused him both pain and beatitude. Wojtyła knew existentially what Norwid wrote:

> Eternal future! On the field that is not eternal
> Laughing at weak man
> You place him before a single end — sorrow...
> And a single truth — that he awaits it....[36]

* * *

From his early years, an awareness of what passes away never left Wojtyła. His experience of time spoke to him of passing. But thanks to the presence of great people in his life, this experience spoke to him still more of becoming the One about whom man, the seeker, asks questions. It was precisely Wojtyła's moral experience of man that formed the anthropocentrism of his anthropology, making it theocentric. His anthropocentrism was an anthropocentrism of God. Contemplating the human person, he contemplated God. God spoke to him in his question about the truth of human love and human freedom. God's transcendence and the transcendence of the human person formed the horizon of Wojtyła's anthropological questions.

This transcendence makes it possible for man to exist as *cosmos*

---

35. Cf. Georg W. F. Hegel, *Zasady filozofii prawa*, preface (Warsaw: Państwowe Wydawnictwo Naukowe, 1969), p. 21; originally published as *Grundlinien der Philosophie des Rechts*, translated by T. M. Knox as *Hegel's Philosophy of Right* (New York: Oxford University Press, 1952).

36. Cyprian Norwid, "W Pamiętniku L. A. — Improwizacja," in *Pisma wszystkie*, vol. 1 (Warsaw: Państwowy Instytut Wydawniczy, 1971), pp. 73-74.

(the Greek word means "order"). The moral experience of the human person, of which Wojtyła speaks, is the experience of the cosmic order present in the person because of transcendence. It is an experience of the integration of the human person in transcendence, as well as of his disintegration when he forgets the transcendence present in him.[37] The moral experience of the human person presupposes a metaphysical memory of the Love that begins to reveal itself *(anamnesis)* precisely in this experience.

In the human being who disintegrates because he is alienated from Transcendence, the question of the meaning of life unravels into a "legion" of secondary questions (cf. Matt. 5:9; Luke 8:30) that devastate the human person. The disintegrated human being ceases to be *capax amoris et libertatis* [capable of love and of freedom], and consequently loses the capacity to enter *in communionem personarum* [into the communion of persons]. He does not participate in the building up of the common good. With his acts, he diabolically negates the person, whereas acts ought rather to be symbols and epiphanies of the person.[38] Wojtyła speaks of the person's self-revelation in acts in *Person and Act*. All this is because the person's act is rooted in the truth, in which he participates with the gift of love, faith, and hope. Precisely this rootedness of the person in the truth allows the moral character of his acts not to be reduced to the "game" of so-called free choice.

Human beings who are not integrated by Transcendence cannot manage to be more than individuals cast into life in society as into a prison. They do not believe in themselves. They fall into both spiritual and psychological disturbances of their nature, which have an effect on their body and on their attitude in its regard. They wither away. Aristotle admonishes us, "One should not follow those who advise us to think human thoughts, since we are human, and mortal thoughts, since we are mortal, but as far as possible one ought to be immortal and to do all things with a view to living in accord with the most powerful thing in oneself, for even if it is small in bulk, it rises much more above everything else in power and worth. And each person would even seem to *be*

---

37. Cf. Karol Wojtyła, *Persona e atto* (Vatican City: Editrice Vaticana, 1980), chaps. 3, 5, and 6.

38. In Greek, the verb *symballein*, from which is derived the word "symbol" *(symbolon)*, means to unite, to encounter, to kiss. The adjective "diabolical" *(diabolon)* is derived from the word *diaballein*, to separate or isolate. Wojtyła discusses the revelation of the person in acts in his work, *Person and Act*.

this part, if it is the governing and better part."³⁹ It is upon this "better part," discovered in the human person's moral experience, that Bishop Karol Wojtyła constructed his adequate anthropology.

Professor Wojtyła taught us to accept criticism in such a way that we could reverence more profoundly the truth we were asking about and seeking. One day, he sent me a letter he had received from a Catholic writer who, while praising one of my articles for its creativity in reflection, revealed that it concealed within it the possibility of a heresy. I note in passing that the same article drew the attention of the professor from Moscow mentioned above. After I had read the letter, I asked the Cardinal, "What should I do?" The response was brief: "Nothing, it's enough to know it and keep working." Remembering this experience, I gave him a similar response when he was already Pope. When I conveyed to him information provided by a very credible source, to the effect that Communist secret agents had had great success in penetrating his entourage, he asked me, "I thought so . . . So what do I do?" I said just as briefly, "Nothing, it's enough to know it and be cautious. God will take care of the rest."

We must not form judgments of Pope John Paul II's worth on the basis of his works, which were doubtless great. Rather, we must measure him with the measure of sanctity, that is, his preoccupation to become ever more good, ever more the "image and likeness" of the God who alone is the Holy One. Human greatness is not found in spectacular acts. The acts that reveal the sanctity of the human person are not visibly successful. They reveal only this: that the life of a man — to quote Shakespeare — is not a tale told by an idiot, signifying nothing. The human-divine dimension of human life makes it a difficult tale, but eliminating this dimension would make the tale inhuman, idiotic. Courage is needed to live in time for the eternity that is the meaning of time. Courage is needed to live remembering God's paternal Transcendence, which is present in every human being, in the conditions created by the immanence of his being in the world.⁴⁰

---

39. Aristotle, *Nicomachean Ethics* 1177b and 1178a. Aristotle, *Nicomachean Ethics*, trans. Joe Sachs (Newburyport, MA: Focus, 2002).

40. We can guess at Wojtyła's interior life on the basis of his poetry, especially the first part of the play *Radiation of Fatherhood*, titled "Adam." The section begins with the significant words, "For many years I have lived like a man exiled from my deeper personality yet condemned to probe it"; "Everyone carries in himself an unrealized substance called humanity." Adam "stopped once on the frontier between fatherhood and loneliness," and said, "'I threw off fatherhood like a burden. . . . Did You have to touch

Vir fortis

Acts accomplished "at the crossroads of eternity and the ephemeral" unveil God and man, who tends "beyond history,"[41] in the direction of ever new horizons. The acts of the human person that tend this far change the world.

Sanctity reaches man from this distance of "beyond history," that is, beyond this world. With such sanctity, the true and the good come into the world. The truth that is received, that is, acknowledged, and the good that is accepted, or embraced with love, change the world. *Praxis* that precedes sanctity alienates man and destroys his environment, for it makes the true and the good depend on him. Societies in which human persons are locked into history to the point of not knowing how to get out do justice neither to man nor to the world.

John Paul II thought and existed so heroically in the history of his earthly life that he was free. So free that, when he was asked what single sentence from the Bible he would save if all the rest of Scripture were to be destroyed, he responded without hesitation, "You will know the truth and the truth will set you free" (John 8:32). He thought and lived heroically in history because he sought his source. Like St. Augustine, he wanted to know God and man. The path toward the source bristles with difficulties, for it always leads against the current. But we must not fear the true and the good at their source.[42] The one who fears them, fears freedom. He surrenders to passing circumstances and falls prey to them.

In speaking of the truth that "sets free," John Paul II was not thinking of scientific truth in the modern sense — which does not mean that he undervalued the latter. He realized, however, that modernity values intelligence (*ratio calcolans*, calculating reason) and not wisdom (with which the *intellectus* is bound in friendship). For this reason, modernity does not want to acknowledge any but scientific truths. This kind of truth can be reduced to hypotheses and theories. Their effectiveness can

---

my thought with Your knowledge that means giving birth? Did You have to touch my will with the love that is fulfillment? I cannot give birth in this way! In me love never fulfills itself. That is why You were disappointed in me. It is better for man to remain alone." Karol Wojtyła, *Radiation of Fatherhood*, in *The Collected Plays and Writings on Theater*, trans. Boleslaw Taborski (Berkeley: University of California Press, 1987), pp. 335-37. Another character in this mystery play, Monica, says, "My father's history is in me. . . . I want my daddy on earth, close, very close to my heart. . . . My father, I am fighting for you. Be in me, as I want to be in you" (pp. 344-46).

41. Ludmiła Grygiel, "I santi e la storia," *Il Nuovo Areopago*, no. 1 (1983): 92.

42. Cf. John Paul II, *Crossing the Threshold of Hope*, p. 6.

be verified experimentally and determines whether they are accepted or rejected. Modern society allows theories that have not yet been rejected to function as if they were "the" truth. Subjecting itself to these theories, society ostracizes all those who live the fundamental questions about the supra-historical sense of life in history. It adores the kind of reason *(ratio)* that produces an infinity of questions to which it responds on its own. It does not have the power to ask the question about the Origin and End, about birth and death. When it is not ordered to the fundamental question, "Whence and where? Where do I come from and where am I going?," reason is dismayed. It is overcome by fear when it glimpses the perilous consequences of its own functioning. John Paul II did everything possible to spare humanity the tragic effects of calculations that lack sufficient reflection — all the more perilous the more they are scientifically smuggled into the life of society. He called attention to the fact that human progress does not consist in devoting one's existence to the realization of one's own calculations, but in entrusting oneself to the love of truth, which is not *ad experimentum*. Progress consists in laboriously journeying toward and awaiting this truth.

John Paul II tirelessly admonished us not to identify license with true freedom and comfort with dignity. Comfort (in Italian, *agiatezza*) is a departure from dignity, which man has a care for only when every day he becomes more and more the "great question" (St. Augustine's *magna questio*) about his own Origin and End.[43] John Paul II dedicated the first catecheses of his pontificate to this "great question." In the catecheses, he reflected poetically on why he knew that there is no place for the question of life's meaning or dignity in technical reasoning. There is no place for the *person* in such reasoning, because it lacks the horizon that materializes only where heaven unites to earth. Without this horizon, man does not know what it means to be human. Through technical reasoning, man can be either an end or an instrument. Caught in the web woven by *ratio* [calculating reason] of the history of technical instruments, man forgets his own sovereignty and becomes its slave. And yet he is afraid to escape this web, for he sees the possibility of disaster.

When, in October 1978, John Paul II cried out during the homily at his inaugural Mass, "Do not be afraid! Open wide the doors to Christ!," he wanted to remind us that human life is firmly rooted in the Origin and the End, that is, in the Love that is God; that these roots are in heaven,

---

43. Cf. St. Augustine, *Confessions* 4.4.

which is the meaning of the earth, and in eternity, which is the meaning of time. If they are detached from heaven and eternity, the human person may not fall into material poverty, but he will surely fall into misery. It is this misery that we must fear, not poverty. We live in misery when we don't know where to go.

* * *

We come to know the truth and the good entrusted to our work in the other person who is present to us, the other human being who confesses himself to us. In confessing himself, man indicates to his neighbor a path that leads within time to eternity. Only by following this path does he live as a priest and a king (cf. 1 Pet. 2:9). In John Paul II, the self-revelation of the truth that always occurs in priestly and royal humanity was one with this same self-revelation in the Eucharistic priesthood he received. His humanity — just as the humanity of his teacher, the Servant of God Bishop Jan Pietraszko — was poetical in a priestly way, and priestly in a poetical way. It pointed symbolically "beyond history." The integration of the persons of these two men was achieved by the transcendence of the Origin and End and by his Eucharistic presence on the altar. This integration determined the quality of their lives and pastoral work, that is, the quality of their presence to others.

In this priestly-poetical presence to others, Bishop Karol Wojtyła's philosophy and Bishop Jan Pietraszko's theology were brought to fulfillment. Both welcomed the "gift of God" and transmitted it to others. Proof of this are Karol Wojtyła's *Person and Act* and *Love and Responsibility*, and Jan Pietraszko's homilies.[44] When both of them asked questions about man, they simultaneously asked about God. They clarified the question about man with the question about God; and they clarified the question about God with the question about man.

The question we formulated at the beginning, "Who is John Paul II?," has to be clarified with the question about the God whom he desired and loved. If the truth of the person is revealed in the other person, then it is revealed above all in the Person of God. The question about man leads man out of the misery of his metaphysical solitude. We need an imagination open to the Invisible in order reasonably to ask the question about

---

44. For a theological understanding of Jan Pietraszko, see several volumes containing his homilies, published in Krakow from the 1960s to the present.

visible man. Only the person who has an imagination that extends "beyond history" understands history. In the introduction to the play, *Our God's Brother*, we read, "Between the man and the attempt to penetrate him there runs a line inaccessible to history. For it is characteristic of man in general that it is not possible fully to fathom him historically. Indeed, an extra-historical element in man lies at the very sources of his humanity. And any attempt to penetrate the man is connected with reaching to these sources."[45]

Karol Wojtyła and later John Paul II asked himself the question, "Who am I?" every day, as he heard the question addressed to him, "Who am I, Christ, for you?" I am convinced that God prepared Karol Wojtyła throughout the entire course of his life for the response that Peter gave on behalf of all the apostles to Christ's question, "But you, who do you say that I am?" One does not arrive at the answer to this question through argumentation. To Peter who tells him, "You are Christ, the Son of the Living God," Jesus responds, "Blessed are you, Simon son of Jonah, for flesh and blood have not revealed this to you, but my Father who is in heaven" (Matt. 16:15-17). Bishop Karol Wojtyła probably had a presentiment that God was preparing him for the Petrine confession of faith in the name of the Church, and to confirm his brothers in their entrustment to God. In this presentiment of his own destiny, he probably feared committing the sin of presumption and pride. One day, at the beginning of the 1970s, we were sharing criticisms of an article that had appeared in a Western European Catholic periodical, which argued that those who gave more material aid to the Church than others ought to have more authority in her. I heard Cardinal Wojtyła say, "The time will come when they will ask us for help!" I don't know why, but without reflecting on it, I thought that the Petrine mystery was hidden in him. But on that occasion I did not dare confide this to him.

After his return from the conclave that had elected Alberto Luciani as John Paul I, I said to Cardinal Wojtyła, "I was afraid that you wouldn't come back to Krakow." "Why?" he asked. "Because there wouldn't be anyone for us to lean on in this difficult time." Upon reflecting for a moment, he replied, "Of course you would find someone you could lean on." After I heard these words, it was clear to me that he had been seriously considered as a candidate at the conclave. John Paul I's secretary told me that after the conclave, the Pope confided to persons in his entourage,

---

45. Karol Wojtyła, *Our God's Brother*, in *Collected Plays*, p. 159.

Vir fortis

"The Cardinals did me an injury, because the new Pope should have been someone else. But unfortunately he's not Italian." A few days later, the secretary asked John Paul I who that other Cardinal might be. "He was sitting in front of me at the conclave." Many years later, when that same Monsignor had access to the official documents of the conclave, he could verify that in front of Cardinal Luciani sat Cardinal Wojtyła.

* * *

Cardinal Wojtyła was a poor man, and thus powerful. But he did not show off his poverty. It had a spiritual and aristocratic character, making him free, in possession of himself — *dominus sui*.

He had nothing of his own, sharing even his professor's stipend with needy students. The Communist authorities could find no foothold to blackmail him. Moreover, Wojtyła did not criticize them directly, but left this task to Cardinal Primate Wyszyński. As far as I have understood, the change in Cardinal Wojtyła happened during a men's pilgrimage to the sanctuary of Kalwaria Zebrzydowska in June 1973. I went with him to give a talk to the pilgrims in the basilica. During the Mass, I found myself near the altar, so I could see the Cardinal's face as he gave his homily. At a certain moment, he began to speak in terms that were rather critical but evangelical of the authorities and of the sociopolitical situation in Poland. He spoke very powerfully. It surprised me, because he had never spoken in this way and I had never seen his face look like that. Only once afterward did I see him thus, as Pope, in the famous speech against the Mafia in Sicily. As we returned to Krakow from the sanctuary, I said to him in the car, "I'm very surprised and struck. You've never spoken like that before. What happened?" He answered, "I don't know. During the Mass, when I saw that immense crowd of exhausted people, something entered into me. Then I was no longer I...." He spoke in similar tones during the Corpus Christi procession in 1978 in Krakow. For me, these were signs of what would happen, for in changing a man, God prepares him for new tasks. In this case, the task could only be one: a task that demands of its bearer an almost absolute freedom, and thus an almost infinite poverty.

Every day, the Cardinal responded to Christ's question, "Do you love me?" Wojtyła responded to him with a responsible love, that is, a love responsible for the people entrusted to his care as a pastor. In doing so, he matured toward the threefold response to the question that Christ would ask not just Peter but him, three times in the Sistine Chapel. I repeat, I am profoundly convinced that the Cardinal had a presentiment of his destiny. In some inexplicable way, he knew that God was preparing him for the mission of confirming his brothers in the faith. From his earliest years, Christ asked him "more" than the others (cf. John 21:15-18). Wojtyła constantly heard the demanding call, "Leave everything and follow me!" Leave everything, even the human love that you, Bishop Karol and Pope John Paul II, knew how to sing in such a profound and appealing way in your magisterium.

This human love was precluded so that with his priestly and Petrine service, he might show that love is the greatest and most important gift for the Church and for the world. All the other gifts come "afterward." On October 16, 1978, Cardinal Wyszyński, speaking to Cardinal Léon-Étienne Duval (from Algeria), defined Cardinal Wojtyła in these terms: "He's a mystic, a poet, a pastor, a philosopher, a saint . . . but he's not a good administrator." For my part, I cannot imagine greater praise for a bishop, even if that supposed inability to manage was in fact, in Wyszyński's opinion, an impediment for a papal candidate. In the Church, it is not all the administrative experts who govern, but the law of fairest love, and the administration should be subordinate to this law. All the administrative criteria should be subordinate to this law. Not even Christ was a good administrator; he did not construct ecclesial structures. He simply loved people in truth. That is to say, he governed those who followed him with his presence rich in mercy (cf. Eph. 2:4). When those who govern in the Church do not entrust themselves to Christ and convert to his infinitely merciful presence, they injure the Church independently of the efficacy of their work.[46] Sooner or later, administrators tire out. Only "those who hope in the Lord renew their strength; they shall mount up with wings like eagles, they shall run and not be weary, they shall walk and not faint" (Isa. 40:31). These people will work in a priestly and poetical way to the last day of their life. The essence of John Paul II's governing showed itself in all its beauty in the hour of his agony. The true decisions regarding the things of the Church are made in the Garden of Olives. If they are made in some other place, they negate God and man.

John Paul II was not concerned with appearing intelligent and wise. He desired only to be reborn continually in the love of God present in every human being. Man and the Church need neither another wisdom nor

---

46. Cf. John Paul II, *Dives in misericordia*, encyclical letter, November 30, 1980, no. 13.

another mode of governing. The human person governs himself when he converts, that is, when he is born again in other persons. My experience of John Paul II's governing, just as of Bishop Jan Pietraszko's, is an experience of the greatness of their daily conversion to others. But always, I saw the beauty of their governing from behind, as it were; I saw the traces that they had left, passing by.

These two men governed in the Church by receiving from God the difficult gift of love and freedom and offering it to others. Both fought for this gift, above all with themselves. The gift is kept alive in us if it is continually won, and thus is "written into pages, hidden yet open."[47] Human beings are free when they obey the Spirit of truth in love, when everywhere they adore the Father in the Spirit of truth (cf. John 4:23). The Father's Son addresses each one of them with the call, "Follow me!" It is the Spirit who calls; the flesh can only compel.

Royal poverty, royal love, and royal freedom always serve. Kings govern by serving those whose good is entrusted to their care. God became a man to serve all men and women. Even on the cross, he did not fear that his greatness would be diminished. One day, after the assassination attempt of May 13, 1981, I said to John Paul II, "Holy Father, God used you cruelly for ends he alone knows. He used you very cruelly." The Pope answered me, "Can there be anything more beautiful, especially to a priest, than to be an instrument in God's hands?" Unconsciously, he was probably repeating the words of St. Peter, "Come to him, to that living stone, rejected by men but in God's sight chosen and precious; and like living stones be yourselves built into a spiritual house, to be a holy priesthood, to offer spiritual sacrifices acceptable to God through Jesus Christ" (1 Pet. 2:4-5). With these "living stones," which serve others in a way befitting royal priests, God built up a "spiritual house" on earth.

* * *

The Church, the sacrament of God's presence for us, is the sacrament of our presence for God. It is born in acts in which the person is epiphanically present for another person.[48] People's reciprocal presence for one another creates the space for their salvation, which has its beginnings in

---

47. Karol Wojtyła, "Thinking My Country: I Reach the Heart of the Drama," in *Place Within*, p. 145.

48. Cf. John Paul II, *Crossing the Threshold of Hope*, chap. 27.

persons transfigured by the truth ("the truth will set you free"). This is what happened in Poland when, in Warsaw in 1979, John Paul II cried out, "Lord, send out your Spirit and renew the face of the earth — this earth!" When the Poles stopped being afraid to be present for one another, the truth destroyed the lie of communism in them. Their words stopped being substitutes for the truth and their acts substitutes for the good. Roman Ingarden said of Edith Stein that she never spoke or wrote a single sentence expressing something of which she was not entirely convinced. What Ingarden said of Edith Stein could just as well have been said of John Paul II. It is worth noting that Ingarden's observation about Edith Stein was made in Cardinal Wojtyła's house, at a time when the communist lie — that is, this separation of the words from the content to which they belong — raged outside.

Karol Wojtyła, poet and priest, saw God's presence in man, in the human being's orientation to the Origin and the End. Thus, when he looked at people, his gaze did not come to a halt in them. The words of St. Augustine were very familiar to him: *"Fecisti nos ad te et inquietum est cor nostrum donec requiescat in te."*[49] You created us oriented to you *(ad te)*, and our hearts are restless until they rest in you. In an earlier draft of *Redemptor Hominis*, the encyclical was supposed to open with these words: "My thoughts and my heart turn *ad Christum Redemptorem*, to Christ the Redeemer."

For John Paul II, encounters and dialogue with people formed the space for his encounter with the Truth that is Christ. Every encounter is a gift. It happens in the place and at the moment when a person reveals himself to another person, when one person entrusts himself to another. This is what existing as gift means. In order to be able to live in the encounter, we have to live as a gift. The encounter of persons is not the result of the kind of reasoning that Christ calls "flesh and blood" (Matt. 16:17). The history of faith, understood as the entrustment of the person to other persons, is identified with the history of their encounters and dialogues, not with the history of their reasoning. The human being becomes a person not with argumentation, but by becoming love.

The priest who does *not* live in encounters realizes himself neither as a man nor as a priest, because he does not realize himself as a person. Others cannot encounter one another in him. The Church is not born in

---

49. St. Augustine, *Confessions* 1.1: "You created us for yourself, O Lord, and our hearts are restless until they rest in you."

Vir fortis

him. In the priest Karol Wojtyła, people with different inclinations and worldviews encountered one another. In his desire for the truth and incessant search for it with his whole being, he became a house open to all. Even atheists felt at home in him, provided that they obeyed their desire for something more than personal success. The priest Karol Wojtyła went in search of this desire in them, and reawakened it in everyone. For him, every human being represented a priceless good precisely because of this desire. In the 1970s, at the death of a famous Jagiellonian University professor whom Wojtyła had known before the war, the professor's daughter asked him to take part in the funeral. The Cardinal asked her, "Did your father believe in God?" "He fluctuated a bit in his religious practice and in his relationship with the Church," the daughter replied, "but he always believed in God." Then the Cardinal answered, without hesitation, "That's enough for me. I'll come." The Communist authorities never forgave him for this decision.

For Wojtyła, every human being is a tabernacle in which Christ is hidden. For this reason, he always asked his questions about man in the light of the Eucharist. He treated everyone with the deepest reverence, convinced that he was thus reverencing God present in man and not the circumstances that made this or that person important in society. He knew the truth about man, thanks to his conversations with the One who knows what is in man and does not need to ask this of anyone (cf. John 2:25).

Karol Wojtyła lived from the people to whom he had entrusted himself, not from opinions about them. Opinions cover up people so that they can no longer be seen. Wojtyła lived above all from the Person of Christ present in man and on the altar, and not from opinions about this Presence in our midst. His thought identified itself with lived reality, and his experience identified itself with thought about this reality. He never treated his own humanity or priesthood as something given *ad experimentum*. The Eucharistic priesthood rooted itself in his humanity, throwing into relief his natural, royal priesthood. Some say that a man must first be a man, and only then a priest. I understand what they mean. But Wojtyła's person, like Pietraszko's, keeps me from agreeing. The humanity of these two men was realized in their priesthood, and their priesthood in their humanity. "I think that to be a pastor means to know how to receive everything that others contribute and the burdens that others carry. To know how to receive means to know how to give — to know how to coordinate, to put things together so that the common good of all may grow. Because each one of us has his or her place in the economy of salvation, each one of us is a great treasure."[50] Each one, without exceptions. The rain falls and the sun shines on the just and the unjust in equal measure. The just and the unjust form the common good not only of the Church, but of society. God gave all human beings a humanity oriented to the Divinity. The priest who forgets this contradicts his priesthood and his humanity.

Bishop Wojtyła cultivated the field of the truth that in some way even the unjust desire. He had time even for them, waiting patiently in hope that one day, the truth would free them from evil. Every human being represented to him a value greater than time. Time is given so that love for man, that is, for his person, might grow in the service of others. Bishop Wojtyła did not think he was wasting time by dedicating it to people, who often came to him with problems that were not very important. For him, what mattered was the person, not the problem. He feared wasting, not time, but those temporal acts that are not oriented to the God who was present in the person coming to see him. Precisely for this reason, all ambition or careerism was foreign to him. He was not interested in horizontal transcendence. His thoughts and his heart looked to vertical Transcendence. This does not mean, however, that he was naïve. On June 6, 1979, he said to a group of priests in the cathedral of Częstochowa, "The easiest way to defeat the Church ... is through priests." In his Holy Thursday letter to priests that same year, he wrote: "If we have the duty of helping others to be converted, we have to do the same continuously in our lives." I spoke with him once about this problem while we were still in Poland. His voice shook with the pain of compassion. This *compassio* was the source in him of a difficult *communio* with those with whom he suffered: those who did not know why they were priests. Such caricatures of the priesthood saddened him, but he sought an adequate place in the Church even for them, since the Church is a communion of sinners.

*　*　*

An awareness of death penetrated Karol Wojtyła's thoughts and heart from his earliest youth. The painful experience of the death of his mother,

---

50. Karol Wojtyła, address given as archbishop upon taking possession of his diocese, Wawel Cathedral, Krakow, March 8, 1964. Cf. Boniecki, *Kalendarium*, p. 216.

sister, brother, father, and friends killed by occupying forces, and the reflection that sought to give this experience rational form, crystallized in the poem, "Meditation on Death." The poem reflects on "maturing toward difficult encounters."[51] Meditating on death and maturing toward it, Wojtyła returned to what was past and nevertheless continued to exist. And he set out toward "the One/in whom existence finds all its future."[52] Every day, the human being passes from "today" to "tomorrow" through the darkness of night. In death, an annihilation takes place, and at the same time a new creation. Existing oriented toward death, man exists oriented toward the future. "Passing through death toward life is a mystery."[53] For this reason, we do not understand death, but in its invisible light everything becomes clear — because the light is paschal.

Karol Wojtyła's "Meditation on Death" helped me to live more religiously and thus more metaphysically. I remember one December evening in 1974. The Cardinal and I were walking through Krakow along snow-covered streets, exchanging thoughts on this poem, which had not yet been published. We stayed in the park we had entered so as to be alone, conversing until midnight.[54] We spoke with words filled with silence more than with concepts. We talked for a long time of the annihilation that one had to pass through in order to be able to be reborn and to be.

> But death is the experience of the limit,
> it has something of annihilation,
> I use hope to detach my own self,
> I must tear myself away
> to stand above annihilation.

51. Karol Wojtyła, "Meditation on Death: Thoughts on Maturing," p. 153.
52. "Meditation on Death: Thoughts on Maturing," p. 154.
53. Karol Wojtyła, "Meditation on Death: *Mysterium Paschale*," p. 156.
54. It is worthwhile to remember what happened that evening in the Krakow park. Meditating on death (on the occasion of the still-unpublished poems, "Meditation on Death" and "Thinking My Country"), we lost our sense of time. When we decided to leave, we found the gates locked. The park custodians had not noticed our presence among the plants. I was worried about my wife. She knew who I was with, but in those days the strangest things could happen. There was no way of telling her that we were alright. The cardinal noticed my anxiety and calmed me, saying, "Don't be afraid. I know that here in the fence there's a hole, we can get out through it!" And that's what we did. This hole in the fence became for me an ever-clearer symbol of the coming Passage — of the Pasch.

And then from all sides they call and will call out:
"You are mad, Paul, you are mad."
I wrestle with myself,
with so many others I wrestle
for my hope.
No layer in my memory alone
confirms my hope,
no mirror of passage recreates my hope,
only Your paschal Passage,
welded to the deepest record of my being.

And so I am inscribed in You
by hope,
outside You I cannot exist.[55]

From the "Meditation on Death," we move to a poem written by Cyprian Norwid after a visit to the dying Frederick Chopin:

I visited you in those days but last
Of life's inscrutable thread —
Full — like Myth,
Pale — like dawn ...
— When life's end whispers to its beginning:
"I won't destroy you — no! — You I'll enhance! ..."[56]

God "enhances" man in the paschal Passage, that is, in the passage of his already created being *(creatum)*, through the emptiness of nothingness, to the being that must still receive "weight," must still be "enhanced." Man is reborn in the experience of love — the experience that is God creating paschally ("enhancing" him), giving him weight. In this passage, the smallest fragment of being shows how great is the power of the true and the good *(verum et bonum)*. With their beauty *(pulchrum)*, they trace out the path that leads man to God. Just as the Servant of God Jan Pietraszko, Blessed John Paul II was a beautiful paschal epiphany of the true and the good for those who encountered and are still encounter-

---

55. Karol Wojtyła, "Meditation on Death: Hope Reaching Beyond the Limit," in *Place Within*, pp. 162-63.

56. Cyprian Norwid, "Chopin's Grand Piano," in *Poems*, p. 69.

ing him in their lives. In both these persons, a great paschal metaphysics took place.

* * *

Karol Wojtyła's adequate anthropology "happened" in his priestly reverence for man — in other words, in his entrustment of himself to God's Transcendence present in man. The thought that creates such an anthropology must have a poetic structure, since it must seek the Source of the true and the good. Together with the beautiful which they reflect, these transcendentals orient Wojtyła's fundamental question regarding the human person, as well as his words and actions, toward heaven. John Paul II's thought and life form a unity in the "image and likeness" of the unity of the Word and Act of God[57] — the God whom the young Wojtyła called "Father of great Poetry."[58]

An adequate anthropology germinates in the moral experience of the person who affirms that the true and the good have enough power to fill man with enthusiasm and to oblige him to work, insofar as they manifest themselves in the beautiful. Karol Wojtyła's anthropology is rooted in the experience of the person integrated by the "gift of God" that is the beautiful *(charis)*. Reverencing man, Wojtyła reverences the "gift of God" that permeates him. It is, consequently, very difficult to indicate the dividing line in his vision of the human person, or where this reverence for man who burns for God passes over to become a profound reverence for God. The Name of God, "I AM WHO I AM," is revealed in the flame that blazes in the burning bush of the human person. John Paul II's thoughts and actions burned with God. Here we find the reason why people were more attached to his person than to his writings. Everyone wants to attach themselves to the truth, to the good. Everyone admires their beauty, which calls them to the freedom without which human life will never be poetry. And only this beauty enraptures even God, to the point that he saves those who have become it.

In his *Letter to Artists*, John Paul II wrote, "Every genuine artistic intuition goes beyond what the senses perceive and, reaching beneath reality's surface, strives to interpret its hidden mystery. The intuition itself springs from the depths of the human soul, where the desire to give

---

57. Cf. John Paul II, *Letter to Artists*, April 4, 1999.
58. Karol Wojtyła, "Magnificat," in *Place Within*, p. 185.

meaning to one's own life is joined by the fleeting vision of beauty and of the mysterious unity of things."[59] We hear in these words an echo of the "Spiritual Canticle" of St. John of the Cross, which Wojtyła analyzed in his work, *The Doctrine of Faith in St. John of the Cross*:

> O crystal well!
> Oh that on Your silvered surface
> You would mirror forth at once
> Those eyes desired
> Which are outlined in my heart![60]

* * *

Only in the prophet and the priest, and to a certain extent also in the poet, powerful thoughts arise that neither time nor space can arrest and destroy. The prophet and the priest speak the language of symbols, each in his way. Each is the contemporary of the other, and they share a single dwelling place. They encounter one another even when they are far apart. They encounter one another in the deepest strata of their persons, where every human being is "a high priest unaware,/And unformed"[61] — because he is not yet fully rooted in eternity.

The words with which Bishop Karol Wojtyła and later John Paul II posed the question about man and thus served him, were words of the "high priest unaware." At the same time, they were words of the priest of the Eucharist. With the poetry proper to the priest still unaware, he asked and sought the Origin and the End of the human person. With the poetry proper to the priest of the Eucharist, he daily indicated the only path that leads to the Answer to this, man's most important question. In the Eucharist, John Paul II saw the "center of the universe and of history,"[62] the Origin of both and their End.

In the catecheses given during the Wednesday audiences, he told the story of man's journey along the winding path that joins the lost and the promised Paradise. What suggested the words to him? Love. And the commandment written from eternity in man's heart, defended in the

---

59. John Paul II, *Letter to Artists*, no. 6.
60. Cf. Karol Wojtyła, *Metafisica della persona*, pp. 187-88.
61. See note 7.
62. John Paul II, *Redemptor hominis*, 1.

Vir fortis

Decalogue on Sinai and confirmed by the Beatitudes Christ proclaimed on the mountain. With poetical language, Pope John Paul II reawakened in human beings a memory of the fact that in prehistory, they begin to be in the Word of God. Thus the desire of their heart finds fulfillment in the post-history that is the same Word. The person who does not remember where he comes from also does not remember where he has to go. He remains confused at his own life, paralyzed before the view of the grave that looms ever more clearly, where, it seems to him, this "tale told by an idiot" ends.

Poets, prophets, and priests speak of death and of the suffering that pervades those who look death in the face. But they speak of this so as to reawaken man from the "sleep" in which, left to himself, he lives in the shadows of the true, the good, and the beautiful. They introduce him into a life in which other people are present. People who are present resist him with the truth for him. This truth is revealed in them and compels him to be similarly present to them. The beauty of the truth that transcends the world reminds man that he comes from and is going beyond history. It reminds him that he must awaken and walk toward the great Encounter. The poetic consciousness of the "priest unaware" and still more the poetic consciousness of the priest of the Eucharist help the human person to understand the history of his being in the world. I don't know whether Norwid was consciously developing the thought of Aeschylus — "We suffer in order to understand" — and of Hesiod — "Suffering restores man to reason" — when he wrote, "With emotion I recall that Socrates, feeling the pain of the chains that fettered his legs, sought to draw profit from it by investigating pain's relation to life. He did not yet and could not know clearly what he was doing. . . . It's time that we know clearly that the greater part of oppressions come because truth and the knowledge of it are not obstructed."[63]

John Paul II never ceased reminding us that where people "obstruct" truth and the knowledge of it, freedom is obstructed in them. Consequently, they lose the capacity to distinguish good and evil. Only those who are responsible can distinguish these — that is, only those who respond to the call of Love. In *Person and Act*, Karol Wojtyła wrote of the truth of man and of his freedom. This freedom is self-possession, that is to say, one's capacity to give oneself to others, when their love calls one

---

63. Cyprian Norwid to Marian Sokołowski, August 2, 1865, in *Pisma wszystkie*, vol. 9 (Warsaw: Państwowy Instytut Wydawniczy, 1971), p. 184.

to be love. Wojtyła sings the dramatic beauty of truth and freedom in the poem, "Thinking My Country." The desire for the true, the good, and the beautiful lead us to the act of creation, in which God sees that everything to which his eyes grant the spark of existence is very beautiful and very good. This desire leads us to the Last Judgment, in which it will become manifest whether the human person has done justice to Love. In communion with the Gaze *(theos)* of God, Karol Wojtyła made of his life's story a work of art. He sought to make it a worthy response to the Love that, with the beauty of Love's Word, called him to work "for his resurrection." In every beautiful work of art, but above all in that work which is the man who is truly human, the eternal, invisible beauty of God becomes to some extent visible in time. He is reflected in the time that is man's history, as the starry sky is reflected in the waters. In the End, we will see how muddied this reflection was in our waters.

Freedom cannot be possessed as we possess the objects we purchase. We must fight for it every day. In the same way, we must fight for love and for its beauty, for the truth and for the good. It is easy to lose them and with them, to lose ourselves. "You pay for freedom with all your being, therefore call this your freedom, that paying for it continually you possess yourself anew."[64] The ancient epigram that asks about the truth — *quid sit veritas?* [what is truth?] — ought to be extended to the question about freedom — *quid sit libertas?* [what is freedom?]. The response should be: *veritas atque libertas sunt vir qui adest* [truth and freedom are the man who is present]. Truth and freedom come to pass in the prophetic *adsum!* [I am present!] of person to person, that is, in their reciprocal *parousia*. In it, the *parousia* of God comes to pass for all men. Through the communion of the reciprocal presence of human beings, the path leads to the Father's communion with his filial Word. That is, it leads to the Origin of the truth and freedom that take place in history, and to the End in which history finds its fulfillment.

"Freedom has continually to be won, it cannot merely be possessed. It comes as a gift but can only be kept with a struggle. Gift and struggle are written into pages, hidden yet open."[65] Everyone has received the priceless gift of life, and the even more precious gift of truth and of freedom. The drama of every human being plays itself out in the tension between the gift of life and the gift of freedom. We have to pay for the gift of

---

64. Karol Wojtyła, "Thinking My Country: I Reach the Heart of the Drama," p. 145.
65. Wojtyła, "Thinking My Country: I Reach the Heart of the Drama."

truth and of freedom with the gift of our life. With nothing else, because everything else has a determinate price. Thus giving one's life for truth and for freedom is inseparable from heroism. In the latter, the beauty of the human person — this "priest unaware" — reveals itself. In a particular way, this beauty is revealed in the heroism of the priest of the Eucharist.

"Truth is the form of love," John Paul II said once to the young people during the first World Youth Day (June 28, 1983). Truth is the beauty of love. Like love, truth is expressed through kingly work, that is, through the service of others, and with a kingly silence more than with words. So we must not marvel if the people who live thus as kings, that is, who love and serve others in kingly silence, do not bow before politics or economics. They give up everything that has a quantifiable price in exchange for the truth, freedom, and beauty that alone can console man, kindling in him the hope of losing nothing of what he paid to have them in the end. He will receive a hundredfold (cf. Matt. 19:29).

The beauty of the true and the good, borne by love, entrusts itself to simple people. It entrusts itself to the learned only when they "forget" their erudite constructions and return to the simplicity of what is priceless. Once, in the late afternoon twilight, I was listening to Chopin's Nocturnes with my mother, a simple peasant. When the music stopped, she said to me, "This music is so sad that it can console even a sad man." At such moments, the universe evolves in the human person according to the laws conceived in the mystery of the Origin. They are moments in which God unveils to human eyes a fragment of his beauty, which gives life both meaning and priceless worth. For such paschal moments of beauty, John Paul II wrote his adequate anthropology. He wrote it as a man and as a priest above all with his life. Only in a second instance did he write it with words.

CHAPTER 2

Via pulchritudinis — *via crucis*

John Paul II surprised not only theologians and clerics, but even laypeople when he began his pontifical teaching with meditations on the beauty of the human body. The "heirs" of the 1960s sexual revolution expected a radical change in the Church's vision of man. A change clearly took place, but that revolution came out of it all the weaker.

John Paul II spoke of the beauty that appears in this world and in us, in our bodies, but that comes from beyond the world and us, revealing our symbolical nature. This beauty appears in our passing world and makes the world a path on which we must set out — if we wish — so that our life can have a meaning and worth that transcend the possibilities of our industrious human "making." We cannot invent this meaning and worth, which open out onto symbolical existence and symbolical thought, not to their diabolical substitutes. To exist and to think symbolically means to live and to think with so great a desire to encounter another person that when we do encounter him, we think and live still more from yet another encounter: the encounter with God. To those who think and who live in the desire for this encounter, every being reveals itself as truth and goodness. It is as if they sense and see in every being that *bonum, verum, et pulchrum convertuntur* — the good, the true, and the beautiful are convertible.

Such people look on themselves and the world as symbols pointing to a reality that transcends them. From it emanates the light thanks to which they can understand themselves and the world. A friendship with wisdom, *filosofia*, is born in them, in their symbolical life just as much as in their symbolical thought. The friend of wisdom does not only see beings, including himself, as they are here and now. He glimpses something through them. He sees that they point to another reality that differs from all of them. This reality is linked to the possibility of another way of being human and, consequently, to the possibility of a totally different way of thinking and knowing. In the eyes of the human person transfigured in his being and thinking, the world, too, exists in a different way. He then speaks of himself and the world with a new and totally different language, a language of poetry and silence.

The truth and the goodness of every being reveal themselves in the form of the beautiful. As Norwid says, the beautiful makes us eager to work. That is, it makes us eager to know every being as truth and to love it as good. The person who lives in friendship with the beauty of the true and the good, the philosopher, seeks the Source from which these transcendentals flow. He experiences the Source present in them, even if he does not experience it directly. The philosopher experiences the Source's presence in its nonpresence. Precisely the language of symbol and silence — which is what poetry is — points to this presence in nonpresence.

Poetry is the human being's response to the beautiful that fascinates, and that calls him as if it belonged to him. The beautiful does not compel us; it begs us to draw near, advancing in the direction it shows us. Obediently, we set out, going much further than the particular being in which the beautiful entered into dialogue with us. "Beauty is a key to the mystery and a call to transcendence. It is an invitation to savor life and to dream of the future."[1] Poetry and silence express man's dream of another life.

The language that the beautiful speaks, and the language with which the human person speaks of the beautiful, transcend the matter of words, colors, and sounds, even if these languages always take form in such matter. The content borne by these languages cannot be reduced to constructions of the human mind. The Source of the beauty that flows like a torrent through man and the world, transfiguring them, is in some way present in it. The human person called and transfigured by beauty does not feel alone and abandoned in the world. Someone has visited him and invited him to Himself. The call with which the beautiful speaks to man helps him to pass from solitude to a marvelous dwelling place of the beautiful, in which everyone can be himself because he feels at home. The Source of the beautiful that transfigures the human person can only be God.

---

1. John Paul II, *Letter to Artists*, April 4, 1999, no. 16.

Beauty has a paschal and therefore a priestly power. It binds together both the riverbanks, human and divine, between which it flows. It calls the human person to life in the divine-human dialogue — a dialogue that consists in the response of his beautiful human love to the beautiful Love that is God. For now, they speak to one another from a distance. One day they will meet face to face. Man's hope is full of this encounter.

Love is always fulfilled in the encounter. Even the Love that is God takes place in the Trinitarian encounter of the Persons. The encounter of persons begins and is accomplished in wonder, without which it would never occur. I close a book if it does not make me eager to work with its author; I can't manage to understand it. It may have fascinated me in the beginning, but a little while later my wonder is spent. The book has become a burden to me. Fulfillment takes place in the greatest wonder. It's not a given that everything that begins must come to fulfillment; things disappear as soon as wonder ceases. With a beauty that makes us eager, love opens the door to the knowledge that unites us to everything that is true and good. Knowledge bereft of wonder degenerates into calculation.

This kind of encounter cannot be constructed. We have to know how to wait for it. We have to mature toward it. It is a gift — a grace. It can't be sought with the conceptual operations of reason. The gift comes from beyond these. It reaches and enraptures people with its own beauty, so that they convert to it and become this gift for one another. Persons fascinated by the beauty that flows through them give themselves, revealing themselves to one another. Thanks to this mutual revelation, they see themselves and know one another. In other words, people know themselves inasmuch as, fascinated by the beauty that reveals their love, they change their lives. Their lives become the content of beauty and of love. Precisely for this reason, knowledge is diminished without life, and life without knowledge. We know in the manner that we live, and live in the manner that we know. Without this symbiosis of knowledge and life, friendship with wisdom, or philosophy, will not arise in anyone.

Philosophy thus understood "takes place" dramatically in man. In Norwid's drama, *Cleopatra and Caesar*, Caesar says to Cleopatra,

> It's not easy to become like gods! . . .
> This is a great — because a daily — labor:
> it's easier, Queen — it's a hundred times more comfortable
> to don the high priest's phylacteries once a year,
> to grasp the knife and slaughter the sacrificial animal

and for doing this to receive
the veneration of the great mass of people.²

Love and its beauty do not seek out the masses or receive homage. They seek out those who are magnanimous, entrusting them with the great tasks: to know the beautiful truth and to love the beauty that is good. Only prophets and mystics live from the beauty of the true and the good, that is, from the beauty of the gift. And poets, who tremble because they do not know what they say with their lips, speak of it most adequately.

For beauty is only
the infant of scarcely endurable Terror, and we
are amazed when it casually spares us.
    Every angel is terrible.³

That "terrible angel" places on the lips of prophets, mystics, and poets words that must be spoken unconditionally. The speakers themselves do not understand these words completely, let alone those who hear them. But if these elect were to keep silent, darkness would cover the world so completely that we would be unable to discern a path. Once I had the courage to tell John Paul II that most of the people who listened to him did not understand his catecheses and homilies. "They are physically near you, Holy Father," I said, "but they are far away from what you are saying." He answered me briefly: "It doesn't matter. Some things have to be said. Man first hears the word. Only afterward does he understand."

Slowly, we understand the beautiful truth of the destiny God gives us, because we fulfill it in communion with others. Welcoming our destiny, we welcome and love ourselves and others. If we fail to welcome it, we live as if we do not belong to ourselves and thus are incapable of giving ourselves to others. We are unable to belong to others. If we fail to welcome our destiny, we destroy the gift of freedom that points to our provenance, for "we indeed are his offspring" (Acts 17:28). Freedom is from God. So great is our destiny!

We are born in the beautiful, and we are reborn thanks to the beau-

---

2. Cyprian Norwid, *Kleopatra i Cezar*, act 1, in *Pisma wszystkie*, vol. 5 (Warsaw: Państwowy Instytut Wydawniczy, 1971), p. 54.
3. Rainer Maria Rilke, "The First Elegy," in *Duino Elegies: A Bilingual Edition*, trans. Stephen Cohn (Evanston, IL: Northwestern University Press, 1998), p. 21.

tiful. The beautiful not only forms the beginning of the way; it is itself the way that leads to the love of the good and the knowledge of the true. The beautiful, the "form of love," teaches us to live paschally. That is, it teaches us to die for the love that is greater than our life. It teaches us to live in hope, for it promises that we will be reborn in God's grace, which is worth more than life (Ps. 63:4). The beautiful has only one meaning and one end: the rebirth of the human person in love and for love. Perhaps for this reason, here on earth the beautiful turns out to be totally useless. But this uselessness is indispensable. It makes it impossible to sell the true and the good, which, like the beautiful in which they reveal themselves, are without price. Selling the true and the good causes the truth to cease to be truth and the good to cease to be good. If beauty had a price, the dignity of the human person would lose its foothold in this world. It would be subject to sale. Learning the dignity of the human person at the school of beauty takes a long time; it requires patience and constancy.

> And so, gradually, I learned to value beauty
> accessible to the mind, that is to say, truth.[4]

The separation of calculating reason *(ratio)* from the intellect *(intellectus)* that sees and reads reality has removed the human person from his original experience of reality, which has an Origin and End. It has destroyed poetry in man. Societies that deprive themselves of the intellects of poets, mystics, and prophets condemn themselves to creating only ephemeral meanings and ends for themselves. Those philosophies are sterile, from which the experience of the beautiful has been banished, and which do not seek inspiration in the vision and mystical experience of man and the world. Thoughts, the contents of which can be contained in a dictionary, do not have the power to lead the human person where he can become more than he already is.

Karol Wojtyła was aware of the sterility that threatens any philosophical thought that distances itself from the beautiful, and therefore also from the experience of love. He did not hesitate to immerse his thought in beautiful love. Despite the criticism that he treated poetry as if it were philosophy, or that he diluted philosophy with poetry against every indication of method, he did not change his attitude before the beauty of

---

4. Cf. Karol Wojtyła, *The Jeweler's Shop*, trans. Boleslaw Taborski (San Francisco: Ignatius, 1992), p. 25.

the true and the good. He remained faithfully firm in the human person's original experience. He did not betray his prophetically mystical and prophetically poetical vocation. He was not an erudite man, it is true. In recompense he was a friend of the wisdom that cannot be attained by erudition. Wisdom can be attained only by love.

In the erudite man, the transcendentals — the true, the good, and the beautiful — are not events. They are objects constructed by his reason, usually borrowed from other erudite people and registered in his memory. He hands these objects on to others, burdening their memory with useless ballast that is soon thrown overboard if it is not registered anew every day. He treats the transcendentals as if they were his property, while they cannot be possessed. The human person must become that which he receives from them. For the transcendentals to "happen" in him, man must have the courage to live in the encounter with other human beings and with God, the Father of the beauty that flows through them. The true, the good, and the beautiful that do not point us a little further, to the transcendent Source, function so diabolically that they make us forget our dignity, a source of inestimable worth. We are content, then, with having a price that changes every day. Kant's distinction between price and dignity formed Karol Wojtyła's reflection on man.

The beautiful, the true, and the good "happen" in man, but they cannot be explained completely by his action. They come to him as a gift; reason does not have the power to take possession of them and turn them into objects of his "making." The metaphysics of the events of the beautiful truth and the beautiful good liberate man from himself and carry him upwards. On the other hand, the metaphysics of erudition (if such a thing is possible) only serves him to a certain limit. It keeps his feet bound to the earth. But one cannot remain thus bound forever. On earth, we prepare for that which is above, toward which we must begin to a certain extent to raise ourselves.

The man or woman in whom the beautiful truth and the beautiful good come to pass burns with the Love whose "form is the beautiful" (Norwid). The metaphysician burns with God. The anthropology of the burning bush on Mount Horeb — or, if you prefer, the adequate anthropology of John Paul II — transcends the science of the human person reduced to predicates. The friend of wisdom continually liberates himself from predication. He remains in the original experience of his own "I am," in the hope that, tempered in the fire of love, it will be transformed. Not into ashes, but into the diamond, whose name is "I AM WHO I AM" (cf. Exod. 3:4-15). Karol Wojtyła writes in *Person and Act* that transcendence integrates the person who moves toward it and awaits it with his body and spirit. Transcendence integrates those who burn with and for it. Friendship with wisdom happens in the "I am" of the human person oriented to God and on fire with his "I AM." Wojtyła's existential philosophy is "on fire" with God and man.

Wisdom transfigures people astonished by the beautiful, people who follow the path traced out by it and who wait for that of which this beauty is the promise. They travel this path and wait for the Promise in the space of good and evil, truth and the lie, joy and sorrow, sickness and health, life and death. In this morally dramatic dualism, they find help in the memory (Plato's *anamnesis*) of the beauty of the pure good, pure truth, pure joy, pure health, pure life. We don't know where to find these immaculate ideals. Doubtless not on earth. And yet they must be somewhere, perhaps in heaven, if earthly life cannot be reduced to a senseless competition for space between one person and another, and between people and things (this is how every form of imperialism behaves).

John Paul II spoke of the memory of man's prehistory and posthistory when, in his first Wednesday catecheses, he read with us the biblical story of the Origin and End in the light of the human person's experience. In the good and the beautiful — which are synonyms in the book of Genesis — is revealed the unity of Love and Work in God. In the act of creation, God assigned to man the task of realizing this unity as the content of his destiny (cf. Gen. 1:28), so that in the way proper to him alone, he might become an ever more beautiful "image and likeness" of God. God did not completely bring to fulfillment either the beautiful or work. He works "even now" (John 5:17). He is the "Father of great Poetry,"[5] which is his only-begotten Son. Man awaits the "voice" that both entrusts this Poetry to him as a task and promises to bring it to fulfillment in him. The promise and the task make the human being a moral being, that is, one who is able to generate and create works of art in the image and likeness of the divine generation and creation. Above all, they make him one who is able to create that work of art which is himself. But he cannot bring this work to completion if he does not co-create it with the "Father of great poetry."

The language of love, which is work performed for the sake of love,

---

5. John Paul II, "Magnificat," in *The Place Within: The Poetry of John Paul II*, trans. Jerzy Peterkiewicz (New York: Random House, 1994), pp. 185-88, at 185.

and the language of work, which is the love that makes man eager for it, make use of concepts. At the same time, however, they transform these concepts into the poetry of metaphors, symbols, and mythical accounts. All of these point to a reality so "other" that it cannot be expressed by any concept closed into its content. Poets open up a closed human language; they enable its matter to stop being matter.

God does not reveal the meaning and value of human life with concepts but with his Word, which is his Poetry. In this Poetry is found our Past (Origin) and Future (End). Thanks to the question, "Where do we come from and where are we going?," works of art have a power that frees us from history. This is true even though they remain dependent on the passing circumstances in which we create them. Works like these remind us that history does not have the last word about man. Someone else will "stand upon the earth" (Job 19:25).

In the perspective of the Poetry that is the Father's Word, I see Karol Wojtyła's adequate anthropology as built on the basis of moral experience, which in its essence is poetic experience. An adequate anthropology comes to pass in the human person when his earthly "here" joins with the heavenly "there." Moral experience would not occur if heaven were not united to earth in him. The morality of the act reveals that the act is related to something that is not this act. This morality interprets the act accomplished "here" in the light of what is "there." Thanks to the meeting of heaven and earth in man, his moral act reveals the truth of the human person and opens the way to fulfillment. The poem that the human person is in God's plan has its sources on earth and in heaven. Every human being is called to make of himself a work of art on earth. That is, he is called to set out on the path that leads to the "Father of great poetry" — to God. I think that ultimately, this, too, is what Wojtyła's *Person and Act* is about.[6]

John Paul II sought the limit of man's self-understanding in the greatness of the human heart that desires truth. And he sought the limits of this greatness of the human heart in the immensity of the Word of the living God. This is the reason why the Pope's teaching cannot be completely identified with his writings. The most important "text" in his teaching was his person. John Paul II proclaimed the Word of the living God with his own life. He made his life a word that bore witness to the Word, the "center of the universe and of history." His person itself was

---

6. See note 2 of chap. 1.

an "adequate anthropology," which is why people adhered more to John Paul II's person than to his texts. People do not live from abstractions.

The work of art is born in human suffering. Man struggles with the material of sounds, words, colors, and forms so that they might be not only sounds, words, colors, and empty forms. He struggles to give a name to matter, just as Jacob wrestled with the angel of God to obtain a blessing for himself — that is, to be "well said" *(benedictio)* as a person. The patriarch wrestled in wonder and in the suffering provoked by the beauty of his own name. As he discovered, matter resists this name, which is the proper "form of love." When, at daybreak, Jacob understood himself in the vision — when he understood that his proper name is love — he began to limp in the logic of this world and gave gifts to his brother Esau, against whom he had wanted to wage war. In these gifts, he brought Esau himself. Jacob died to himself to rise in his brother.

The struggle to give a name to matter weakens any artist. It weakens beyond measure the artist who struggles for the blessing of the material of his own being. This struggle exhausts man. It even destroyed the humanity of the Only-Begotten Word of the living God. The people exhausted by this struggle are works of art more beautiful than those found in museums. The most beautiful poem on earth is the exhausted humanity of Christ. In the play *Our God's Brother*, written by the young Karol Wojtyła, Brother Albert Chmielowski addresses these words to Christ, whom he contemplates in a painting Brother Albert himself painted, *Ecce Homo*:

> They have exhausted you. . . .
> But with all this you have remained beautiful.
> The most beautiful of the sons of men.
> Such beauty was never repeated again.
> Oh what a difficult beauty, how hard.
> Such beauty is called Mercy.[7]

In the beauty of every work of art, there is a touch of mercy. The mercy of the Beauty accomplished in the "exhausted" humanity of the Son of the living God, the difficult Beauty of merciful Love, saves the

---

7. Karol Wojtyła, *Our God's Brother*, in *The Collected Plays and Writings on Theater*, trans. Boleslaw Taborski (Berkeley: University of California Press, 1987), p. 227 (translation slightly altered).

world (Dostoyevsky). It makes man similar to itself. In this "making similar" on the part of God, I see the very essence of divine Mercy.

Rationalist scientists do not know mercy because they do not know what beauty is. When they speak of it, they refer to something else. They do not unite their work to love. For this reason, they do not create works of art. Their Promethean *praxis* divides the earthly "here" from the heavenly "there." And experience teaches us that the human person is incapable of facing the beauty that is difficult while trusting nothing but the earth. The sciences will not save man, because Beauty "happens" in the mystery of the drama that he is. This drama unfolds simultaneously on earth and in heaven. Norwid writes,

> If I took off my body
> And unhinged myself from my bones, if I remained
> Carrion in the dust, and my soul still had eyes
> For the world — perhaps I would sing a prophetic hymn
> Aloud — but if I am so weak
> And so small — where will I find the strength
> For this? — Why do thoughts like mercenary scoundrels still
> Blaspheme cruelly and cry that my words,
> My words will pay for them? . . . small golden chimes
> That speak with insipid sound! Broken, false
> Coins! . . . ah! it is an immense poverty and misery
> When even words are lacking, when the soul is
> Dazed and knows not what to do — or perhaps it knows
> Everything — and cries to you, "Help, O God!"[8]

The philosophy that has no place for the twofold presence of the divine and the human in man, passes by the mystery of beauty with indifference. It overlooks the mystery both on the side of earth and on the side of heaven. The Muses flee from an anthropology that erases the memory of the human being's divine origin. They do not forget that they were generated by Memory (Mnemosyne), the daughter of Heaven (Uranos) and Earth (Gaia), whose brother is Time (Kronos). If Time destroys the blood-ties that unite him to his sister, Memory, he wounds the "Father (Uranos) of great poetry" and his *praxis* is rendered sterile.

---

8. Cyprian Norwid, "Do piszących," in *Pisma wszystkie*, vol. 1 (Warsaw: Państwowy Instytut Wydawniczy, 1971), pp. 27 and 28.

So we should not be surprised if John Paul II's poetry, more than all his philosophical texts, introduces us to the vision of man who desires to become God, and of God who also has desired to be man. Only poetry can unveil the mystery of the love — or mercy — that raises man to God and makes God humbly descend to man. Poetry "happens" on this ascending and descending ladder. Any other poetry is only a substitute for poetry. The philosophy that nourishes itself from these substitutes has nothing to do with friendship or with wisdom.

"Art is the language of the human being. It is the language of that being who, before losing himself in the multiplicity of things or allowing himself to be absorbed by countless activities that give us the illusion of living intensely, has the capacity for wonder."[9] Wonder, and the poetry that arises from it, prepares man, who passes away, to live in that which does not pass away. We wonder not at that which passes, but at that which remains. Passing away saddens us. Paul VI said, "This world in which we live needs beauty in order not to sink into despair."[10] Only that which does not pass away defends us from despair. The astonishment and wonder reawakened by beauty open the human person to the order of love (*ordo amoris*), which is the order that endures. Love and love's "form," the beautiful (Norwid), endure. They fill us, who live in time, with enthusiasm and raise us to the eternity in which human time finds its meaning and its worth. The aesthetical metaphysics of beauty reawakens in us the hope that is full of eternity. In this hope, the ethic takes shape that keeps us from losing the memory that,

> Of the things of this world only two remain,
> Two alone: poetry and goodness . . . and nothing else.[11]

The German poet Hölderlin thought as Norwid did:

> Many a man
> Is shy of going to the source;
> For wealth begins in
> The sea. . . .

9. John Paul II, homily at Holy Mass for artists, Brussels, May 20, 1985.
10. Cf. Paul VI, address to artists at the closing of the Second Vatican Ecumenical Council, December 8, 1965.
11. Cyprian Norwid, "Do Bronisława Z.," in *Pisma wszystkie*, vol. 2 (Warsaw: Państwowy Instytut Wydawnicz, 1971), p. 238.

Via pulchritudinis — via crucis

. . . .
    But it is the sea
That takes and gives remembrance,
And love no less keeps eyes attentively fixed,
But what is lasting the poets provide.[12]

The great poets speak of this, even when they claim that they do not believe in the "Father of great poetry." They point to him with words given to them by the desire they serve, since the desire does not come from them. It is not the result of their "unbelief." The great poets listen attentively to the "voices" of love and death; they participate carefully in their own passing and remaining. Societies would be different if, together with the poets, they listened with greater attention to the "voice" of beauty and allowed it to set them on fire. Perhaps they would live in greater material poverty. But they would surely not live in so great an interior poverty, which is the true misery. As it is, they are imprisoning themselves ever more deeply in this latter form of poverty, seduced by substitutes for beauty and happiness.

    That which is beautiful is not . . .
What pleases today, or has pleased,
But what should please; just as
That which is good is not what gives the most pleasure
But what makes us better. . . .[13]

A society entranced by the possibility of producing *homunculi* in a laboratory, by means of scientists who follow in the footsteps of Wagner in Goethe's *Faust*,[14] does not look at the human person as a work of art but as one of many products. Consequently, it does not treat him as the fruit of the work to which the beauty of love calls us, but as an object subject to the rules of market exchange. The human person, treated thus, fears becoming an object of the "making" of those who are stronger than he. So

---

    12. Friedrich Hölderlin, "Remembrance," *Poems and Fragments*, trans. Michael Hamburger, 4th ed. (London: Anvil Press Poetry, 2004), p. 579.

    13. Cyprian Norwid, "Promethidion — Bogumił," *Pisma wszystkie*, vol. 3 (Warsaw: Państwowy Instytut Wydawniczy, 1971), pp. 434-35.

    14. Cf. Johann Wolfgang von Goethe, *Faust*. The *homunculus* is a being produced in vitro by the scientist, Wagner. The latter is inspired by Mephistopheles, the father of lies, who continually divides people from one another, placing them in opposing camps.

until he dies, he does everything in his power to be others' master and not their slave. From conception until death, he struggles against everyone to be some*one* and not something that is thrown out when old or no longer useful. Society realizes too late that in this dialectic, being a master is no different from being a slave.

Beauty gives itself to everyone's contemplation, calling everyone to identify with it. It knows neither master nor slave. It abolishes the master-slave dialectic by uniting everyone in itself without regard to provenance, race, religion, or rank. The beauty in which love reveals itself does not differentiate between persons. Plato continually reminds us that nothing but the beautiful light radiated by the Good draws people out of the cave of alienation. Nothing else frees us from the "shadows" — the opinions and hypotheses *(doxa)* about man and the world that always require experimental proof. In his *Letter to Artists*, John Paul II cites the words of Plato: "The power of the Good has taken refuge in the nature of the Beautiful."[15] In the life of great artists, "art reveals itself as a path that can lead to Christian perfection."[16] This is a perfection to which dialectic remains extraneous.

In Plato's *Symposium*, Diotima tells Socrates that beauty gives meaning and value to human life.[17] The power of the good hidden in the beautiful opens itself to man in the presence of the other. Every human being is a symbol of Man.[18] Every human being is thus a path to Man for others, insofar as the individual lives poetically, that is, symbolically — insofar as he lives "here" for "there." The path of the beautiful begins in the beautiful body and passes through beautiful thoughts and beautiful actions. Finally, it reveals itself to be no longer a new fragment of Beauty, but Beauty itself. On the path toward Beauty — we can call it the *via pulchritudinis* — the true and the good "happen" each time the human person entrusts himself to a fragment of Beauty. This maturation toward the Beauty of the true and the good takes place when we thus entrust ourselves, placing our hope in the consequences of this entrustment. I would define this maturation as *adequatio fidei, spei, et amoris cum Pulchritudine* [the adequation of faith, hope, and love with Beauty]. This definition tells us who Truth is rather than "what" it is.

---

15. John Paul II, *Letter to Artists*, no. 3.
16. John Paul II, homily at the solemn celebration of the Jubilee of Artists, proclaiming Blessed Fra Angelico patron of artists, Basilica of St. Maria sopra Minerva, February 18, 1984, no. 2.
17. Plato, *Symposium* 211b-e, 212a.
18. Plato, *Symposium* 191d.

Via pulchritudinis — via crucis

Beauty makes us eager to work, but at the same time it makes us suffer.[19] It will make us suffer for as long as we struggle to become someone who can be spoken adequately by it *(benedictio)*. Beauty has to make us suffer, for it is not easy to respond every day with dignity to the call to live in the beauty of the body, thoughts, and actions. Our love will always be lacking . . . the love that is able to say to Beauty: Let it be done to me according to your words and not according to my will!

In his *Confessions*, St. Augustine described the *via pulchritudinis*, the way to the Beauty that is God. This path on which we come to know the truth is difficult. On it, every fragment of beauty proclaims the Beauty God promises, yet these fragments also tempt us to rest in them. St. Augustine confesses with conscious sincerity where and why he stopped along the path by these fragments instead of continuing his pilgrimage, trusting in Him who reveals Himself in them only for an instant. Weeping with the joy and happiness that filled her when she saw the Risen One, Mary Magdalene heard the words, "Do not hold me, for I have not yet ascended to the Father" (John 20:17). Jesus will walk with us along the path of beauty's fragments to the Father, until the end of the world.

John Paul II saw how Enlightenment rationalism wished to forget the Beauty of the Origin and the Beauty of the End. The logic of rationalism does not reach as far as the logic of love for the beautiful body, beautiful thoughts, and beautiful actions. In the tragic age of contempt for the beauty of the person — in the years of the Nazi occupation and Soviet domination, but also in his years of study in Western Europe after the war — it became clear to Karol Wojtyła that man's surrender to a nearsighted reason that calculates based on life's circumstances, leads nowhere. Or rather, it leads to so profound a profanation of the beauty of the body, thoughts, and actions that they cease to be epiphanies of the true and the good. He who refuses the gift also refuses the giver. The negation of the "gift of God" is the negation of God and of man. Man is the first and most beautiful gift that God makes . . . to man.

When he was still a young priest, Wojtyła recognized the danger of a profanation of the beauty of the body, thoughts, and actions of the human person. The sacred character of their beauty was revealed to him in the friendships he formed during his university years. It was revealed to

---

19. Cf. Stanisław Grygiel, "Piękno zachwyca i boli . . . (Postscriptum do antropologii adekwatnej K. Wojtyły)," *Oblicza piękna, Sympozja 3*, ed. Czesława Piecuch (Krakow: Wydawnictwo Uniwersytetu Ekonomicznego, 2009), pp. 19-32.

him in the works of the great Polish poets, whose works he recited in the clandestine Rhapsodic Theater, at a time when his compatriots paid for the beauty of the love revealed in their body, thoughts, and actions with life in a concentration camp. Karol Wojtyła knew perfectly well that to Plato's saying, "Beauty is difficult," we must add: it is also dangerous for all those in whom it is revealed.

The sacred character of the beauty of the human person was first revealed to Karol Wojtyła by the love that unites man and woman. This love is fashioned "now" in them, in God's creative work through his Son (cf. Gen. 1:27-28 and John 1:3-4). The humanity of the Son of God was conceived in the beauty of the body, thoughts, and actions of a young Jewish girl. Wojtyła expressed this in two works, which form a single whole. The first is the series of spiritual exercises he preached to artists in Krakow in April 1962, only recently published in Polish with the title, *Evangelization and Art*.[20] The second is the series of catecheses on the beauty of the human body, given by Pope John Paul II. The latter evolved into a description of man's moral maturation on the path that leads him from his Origin to his End. I add immediately that the crowning of these works is the *Roman Triptych*, in which John Paul II asked the fundamental question of the Source (the Origin) and Judgment (the End). His encyclicals and apostolic letters speak of particular moments on man's path. Inspired by translators of the Septuagint, who were faithful to the suggestion of the Hebrew language, he created his own vision of the human person on the foundation of the biblical identification of the good with the beautiful: God saw all that he had made, and it was "good and beautiful."

"To the extent that we think of the Gospel as a living totality, the bonds uniting the Gospel and art appear ever more clearly. These bonds are formed above all because the God of whom the Gospel speaks is Beauty."[21] The Gospel expresses this in various ways. In the dialogue with the young man who addresses Jesus with the words, "Good Master," Jesus observes that only God is good, that is, beautiful.

Bishop Wojtyła followed the suggestion of the translators of the Septuagint, as well as classical metaphysics, which lives from the contemplation of the being that "happens" as the beautiful truth and the beautiful good. He called artists' attention to the fact that we discover beauty in the

---

20. Karol Wojtyła, *Ewangelia a sztuka: Rekolekcje dla artystów* (Krakow: Instytut Dialogu Międzykulturowego im. Jana Pawła II, 2011).

21. Wojtyła, *Ewangelia a sztuka*, p. 26.

totality of creation as well as in the works of man.[22] He based his reflections on the words of Zygmunt Krasiński: "The torrent of beauty flows through you, but you are not Beauty."[23] Bishop Wojtyła adds, "In these words we find a profound self-awareness. . . . Every human being can say this of himself." Every human being is an artist, through whom Beauty flows. We have received a talent that allows this "torrent of beauty" to flow through us. To a certain extent, we are this torrent. We identify with it and are responsible for it.[24] The torrent of beauty that flows through us draws from us what is beautiful and rejects what is ugly and hinders its flow. It does this, however, on the condition that we collaborate with Beauty itself.

"We must accept and acknowledge that of all the talents we possess, the greatest is that of humanity. . . . If God asks us to give an account of how we have used our various talents, he will ask us from this point of view: How have we used that fundamental talent, the talent of humanity? This is the greatest talent. Why? Because God himself paid for our humanity."[25] This price that was paid reveals the meaning of humanity, the value of the work of art that is man.

Not all people are called to paint, to write poems, or compose music. "As Genesis has it, all men and women are entrusted with the task of crafting their own life: in a certain sense, they are to make of it a work of art, a masterpiece."[26] As a person, the artist labors on various works of art, as well as the masterpiece of love and work that is himself (cf. Gen. 1:27-28). He must ask himself two questions every day: Does my humanity keep me from being a good artist? Does my being an artist keep me from being human? Humanity is a hindrance to being a good artist and being an artist is a hindrance to being human only for those who deny the true and the good that reveal themselves in the beauty of beings. Such people bend the bodies, thoughts, and actions of man toward the earth. They submit these to the laws that govern the earth instead of allowing the beauty of

---

22. Wojtyła, *Ewangelia a sztuka*, p. 28.

23. Zygmunt Krasiński, *Nie-boska komedia* (Wrocław: Zakład Narodowy im. Ossolińskich, 1959), p. 3. Karol Wojtyła does not cite a second sentence, which forms a very important part of this thought: *"Vae tibi — vae! —* A child crying on his nurse's breast — the flower of the field that knows nothing of its own fragrance, has more merit before the Lord than you."

24. Cf. Krasiński, *Nie-boska komedia*, p. 36.

25. Krasiński, *Nie-boska komedia*, pp. 38-39.

26. John Paul II, *Letter to Artists*, no. 2.

the true and the good to raise up the bodies, thoughts, and actions of man to the law that governs Beauty itself: the law of disinterested sacrifice.

Beauty does not come from the earth, even though it takes place on the earth; it "happens" only in the person who is in ecstasy toward heaven. It is from "there" that he sees himself and the world, just as the creative Gaze *(theos)*[27] that brings them into being sees them. The person in ecstasy toward heaven unites himself to this Gaze; thanks to it, he creatively contemplates himself and the world. He creates a work of art in his interior that emphasizes the beauty of his person and, in this, the beauty of the earth. Thus bringing God's work to the completion that all creation awaits with eager longing, he reveals himself to be a child of God (cf. Rom. 8:19-21). Let us not forget that in his Son, God works creatively until today (cf. John 1:3; 5:17). He therefore also works in us.

The creator of the work of art, especially of the masterpiece that is his life, will not escape suffering. Hölderlin writes,

> my mind and my heart
> ... paid from the beginning
> In grief for thought and art.
> . . . .
> The deity kindly escorts us,
> . . . .
> With beauty the bubbling source of
> The primal image yields.[28]

The beautiful is difficult and at the same time well disposed toward man. The ecstasy it prompts makes it impossible for him to deny this. He can refuse to receive what it brings with it; he can reject the true and the good. But whoever says that he is not seized by the beautiful in which the true and the good are offered to him is a liar. We reject appearances of the beautiful that only momentarily attract our gaze. The rejection of beauty itself, on the other hand, is identical with the rejection of the love that comes to us in the "form" of the beautiful, with all its gifts. The rejection of the beauty of love, of love's promise and our hope, makes it impossible to know man. It therefore also makes friendship with wisdom — *filosofia* — impossible.

---

27. The Greek word *theos*, which means God, is derived from the verb *theaomai* — I watch, I see — and denotes the gaze.

28. Friedrich Hölderlin, "The Walk," *Poems and Fragments*, p. 755.

Via pulchritudinis — via crucis

To accept the ugliness of the lie and of evil devastates poetry. For this reason, such an acceptance bends man toward the earth in a movement that ends in the secularization of both man and society. Secularized human beings know only what they themselves invent. This is too little to be able to know the person and the world he has received. A knowledge that has been reduced to inventing objects treats everything and everyone as one treats things according to the opinions and fashions of the moment. On the other hand, it is impossible to fabricate the beauty that is reflected above all in the human person; we can only "highlight" or wound it.[29] Transcendence, the source of the torrent of beauty, always remains intact, waiting for those who have strayed from it. This source, and not man, is the Origin and End of our hope.

The body, thoughts, and actions that are bent toward the earth do not receive the Beauty of the Divinity, which reveals itself like a lightning flash at an unforeseeable moment — we have to wait for it. The bolt of lightning frightens those who are bent toward the earth because they are not seized by heaven. They do not invoke it, asking it to open itself and show, just for an instant, the Beauty that dwells "there." They are afraid of heaven.

> Only at times can our kind bear the full impact of gods.
> Ever after our life is dream about them. . . .
> . . . meanwhile too often I think it's
> Better to sleep than to be friendless as we are, alone,
> Always waiting, and what to do or say in the meantime
> I don't know, and who wants poets at all in lean years?
> But they are, you say, like those holy ones, priests of the wine-god,
> Who in holy Night roamed from one place to the next.[30]

So we mustn't be surprised if the enemies of divine and human transcendence bend poetry and philosophy toward the earth, because human beings cannot follow the light that the sudden illumination leaves in them. Their hostility toward God and man explodes in persecution. They kill poets and priests above all, so that the "torrent of beauty" (Z. Krasiński) does not course through the world and revive us. People revived by

---

29. Cyprian Norwid, "Chopin's Grand Piano," in *Poems*, trans. Danuta Borchardt (Brooklyn, NY: Archipelago Books, 2011), pp. 69-77.

30. Friedrich Hölderlin, "Bread and Wine," *Poems and Fragments*, p. 327.

the heaven that enraptures them raise themselves up from the earth. They raise their minds and their wills.

* * *

The poet exists on the earth, but he dwells on the horizon that is traced out in his poetic interior as the fruit of the loving union between heaven *(Uranos)* and earth *(Gaia)*. The poet listens to the "voices" that reach earth from heaven. The word falls upon the prophet, illumining his mind and seducing his will. Thus illumined and seduced by the "voice" of Heaven, he receives the words he must speak to peoples and kingdoms without paying heed to the consequences (cf. Jer. 1:10). The poet's word speaks with the "voice" of enrapturing beauty. The prophet's word, on the other hand, speaks with the "voice" of the moral conscience, which reproaches us for having hearts so hardened *(sklerokardia)* that the poet's words bounce off of them like pebbles against a wall. Prophecy cultivates the earth for God's Poetry. The prophetic conscience is the act of remembering the beauty that has been forgotten, along with its forgotten gifts. Poetry that is composed by one who has forgotten the moral conscience does not sustain being. It is not poetry, for God's Poetry is not present in it.

Until the last moment of his life, Blessed John Paul II spoke with the "voice" of the priest and the poet, who prophetically listens to the "voice" of the moral conscience. This was his contemplation of God's Beauty reflected in the human person. I will never forget a conversation with Cardinal Wojtyła in the garden of the Cistercian Abbey at Jędrzejów, where we had stopped on the way to Lublin for some university lectures. After a morning Mass, we walked along the tree-lined pathways for a long "minute," exchanging just a few words that heightened the silence all around us. "The men who live here contemplate the silence of the beautiful Presence in everything that exists; they can't but perceive the meaning of life," I said. After a moment, the Cardinal completed my thought: "Because this meaning is here."

Prophets, priests, and poets reveal to us that we belong to heaven, that it is our homeland and our refuge. Heaven reveals itself to us in our fellow man, but heaven itself is always a little further. It says to us, "You are mine!" And we answer heaven, "You are mine!" The human person enraptured by heaven receives his identity from it. With his identity, he also receives moral obligations. The experience of moral obligations shows us to whom we belong. Or in Wojtyła's words, we can say, "Mine!"

Via pulchritudinis — via crucis

Man does not need heaven as if it were some object that would make his life easier. He desires heaven. He desires to encounter a person in whom he can dwell as in his own home — or his own country, which is found "on the pathway of blazing stars . . . that like a cascade of creation irrupts from the immense bosom of GOD."[31] Sartre's words, *"L'enfer, c'est les autres!"* ("Hell is other people!"), are a lie. We ought rather to say, *"Le ciel, c'est les autres!"* ("Heaven is other people!")

On pilgrimage toward heaven, man must not even try to remain forever on earth. Conspiring with the earth against heaven, he eliminates the meaning and value of his own life. He does not feel obliged to anything at all. Consequently, he does not know his own rights. He knows only his pretensions. The person who remains bound to the earth is no longer *naturus*, for he cannot find in himself the strength for being reborn. One can be reborn only in another person and, ultimately, in God. The man bent over his own immanence becomes an "idiot" (the Greek word *"idiotes"* means a man enclosed in his private interests). Only idiots reform the circumstances in which they live but are not reborn, for they live in solitude. They are not familiar with the event called *natura*; consequently, they are also unfamiliar with natural laws. To borrow Sartre's image, they are like a broken web tossed about in the wind from one bush to another.

Wojtyła's analysis of the word "mine" demonstrates that the love that is the human person, is a continual returning to those to whom he belongs. The experience of the person's return to the person opens up to the mystery of the reciprocal belonging of the Divine Persons. They belong to one another in such a way that their Love is situated above moral obligations. Defects in persons' belonging to one another in this way force them to depend not only on grace but on ethics.

Following the pathmarks of the "torrent of beauty" as he journeys to the source, man ascends Mount Tabor, where the Love of the "Father of great poetry" transfigures the human material of temporal words, sounds, and colors into the Poetry of his Word. Matter remains here below, and God "extends the column of the voice, like a risen reality rapt in ecstasy into heaven."[32] Heaven places its hand on the hand of the artist who creates the work of art.[33] For this reason, none of the artist's works

---

31. Cyprian Norwid, "Promethidion," in *Pisma wszystkie*, vol. 3, p. 425.
32. Norwid, "Promethidion," in *Pisma wszystkie*, vol. 3, p. 437.
33. In *Letter to Artists*, no. 8, John Paul II cites Dante's words in the *Paradiso*, canto 25, lines 1-2: "If ever it happen that this sacred poem/to which both Heaven and Earth

can fully be identified with his own act of creation. All of his fruits will always be "green," unripe. In Sophocles' tragedies, the dramatist says infinitely more than he thought he said. Man's works of art are born in his dialogue with Transcendence. This is why they are beautiful, but always still incomplete. They offer thoughts that almost touch God's Transcendence — and man's. For this reason, those who contemplate a work of art and enter into dialogue with its artistic creator, also enter, with the artists' help, into dialogue with God. As Roman Ingarden affirms, what is painted is not the same thing as the work the painting wishes to express. This work arises in the collaboration of the person who contemplates the painting with the painter.

The person is the work of art that man co-creates in dialogue with God. This co-creation is the very essence of the spiritual life, without which the beauty of the human person will never attain fulfillment.

Beauty will save man, says Dostoyevsky. But it will save him on the condition that he co-creates beauty in himself with God and with others. The key to the salvation of the person must always be sought in another person, for man is reborn and rises in the other person. The work of art that is the human person, whose fulfillment is the resurrection, does not come into being through argumentation but rather in an artistically creative *praxis*. It can come into being only in a dialogue of persons that transcends the *cogito* of each individual. The resurrection is fulfilled in the gift, and only the person is gift. That is, eternity begins to shine through in the beauty of the true and the good that reveal themselves in persons. Eternity reveals itself in the human fragments of Beauty that Love, who is God, scatters throughout time. Listening to Chopin's music, Norwid wrote,

> *The Host — through the pale wheat I see . . .*
> *And Emmanuel already dwells*
> *On Mount Tabor!*[34]

The beauty of the wheat comes from the Host, not the wheat. The wheat is fulfilled in the Host, when the wheat carries the latter like a gift already present in it.

---

have set their hand." Dante, *Paradise*, vol. 3 of *The Divine Comedy*, trans. Mark Musa (New York: Penguin Classics, 1986), p. 295.

34. Cyprian Norwid, "Chopin's Grand Piano," p. 71 (suspension points original).

Via pulchritudinis — via crucis

* * *

John Paul II never forgot Christ's admonition, "Watch and pray!" The Pope knew that only those who watch and pray create works of art, especially the greatest work of art, themselves. Only they work creatively, because they collaborate with the God who created the wheat and transfigures it in the Host. Only they discern beauty, because they sense that it sees them. The beautiful guards them from coming to a standstill in any fragment of reality: "here there is no place/that does not see you. You must change your life."[35] The beautiful keeps vigil over the freedom and moral conscience of human persons. To the end of the world, this is how it will keep vigil over the process in which they become love.

— Oh, the work of History is not finished,
Conscience has not yet burnt the world to ash![36]

* * *

The world does everything possible so that we will not be enthused by the beauty of the person, for the world fears losing its power over him. Beauty strips the world of its dominion over man. It is impossible to chain people enraptured by the beautiful to the opinions and hypotheses that rule the world. People committed to the beautiful build a home, an *ethos*, for themselves, on the foundation of freedom rather than tolerance. They build it together because they love one another. They do not know what it means to "tolerate" the person. The world does not love beauty and freedom; it does not tolerate them. That is, the world tolerates everyone except those who are free, because it does not tolerate the true and the beautiful. Bishop Karol Wojtyła and then Pope John Paul II confronted this intolerance. He did so in the name of Love and Love's beauty.

In Plato's dialogues, for example *The Republic* and the *Gorgias*, the philosopher wonderfully describes the intolerant intelligence of the modern world. When we read these texts, we have the irresistible impression that the author is speaking to our society today. Plato is our

---

35. Rainer Maria Rilke, "Archaic Torso of Apollo," in *Ahead of All Parting: The Selected Poetry and Prose of Rainer Maria Rilke*, trans. Stephen Mitchell (New York: Modern Library, 1995).

36. Cyprian Norwid, "Socialismo," in *Poesie*, trans. Silvano De Fanti and Giorgio Origlia (Bologna: CSEO, 1981), p. 131.

contemporary. Apart from the circumstances of time and space, nothing has changed from the time of the Athenian democracy he describes until now. As in the myth of the cave, today too, we are dominated by the slaves of opinion and experimental verification. Everything these slaves do, they do *ad experimentum*, demanding tolerance for all their experiments. They entrust themselves definitively to no one and nothing. Entrusting oneself forever to another person frightens them. The word "eternity" strikes fear into them, so they eliminate it from their memory together with moral obligations. Thus they live not according to law but rather according to their claims. People paralyzed by a fear of eternity do not perceive that they are called to anything. They do not say to anyone: I belong to you!

Detached from reality, they reject the intellect that unites us to it. They do not see and read either man or the world (*intellectus — inter legere, intus legere*, to read between [*inter*] or within [*intus*]). They become semi-illiterates who only know how to write the quantities they themselves have calculated. They know only what they themselves write down, and they only write down calculations. Thus they acknowledge and accept only that kind of calculation that is *ratio* (from *reor, reri, ratum* — to calculate). They do not know how to read the writing they receive, which transcends their calculations. Poetry is foreign to them. They forget that each individual is a letter written and sent to him from the "Father of great poetry." For this reason, they write about themselves, their bodies, thoughts, and actions whatever comes to mind about themselves, and are preoccupied only with the efficacy of their writing.

People detached from reality and immersed in calculation do not live the fundamental question regarding the Origin and the End. This question cannot be calculated. Man *becomes* the question, "reading" it from within his own being, which passes away. The question roots him in the Past and the Future, which embrace and comprehend the earth in a way that liberates him from it. People uprooted from reality, that is, uprooted from heaven and consequently also from earth, humiliate themselves. They do not seek the Origin and End in the spirit that breathes life into the "dust of the earth" (Gen. 2:7). Rather, they seek the Origin and End by breathing the "dust of the earth" into themselves.

Bishop Karol Wojtyła in Poland, and then Pope John Paul II in the so-called Western world, went out to meet people humiliated by systems (still) based on the affirmation that there is nothing beyond the "dust of the earth." People who adore the "dust of the earth" presume that they

Via pulchritudinis — via crucis

can obtain their personal dignity by behaving as if they were gods. John Paul II had very much in mind the words of the poet Czesław Miłosz:

> I did not expect to live in such an unusual moment.
> When the God of thunders and of rocky heights,
> the Lord of hosts, Kyrios Sabaoth,
> would humble people to the quick,
> allowing them to act whatever way they wished,
> leaving to them conclusions, saying nothing.[37]

In a rationalistic and *eo ipso* irrational way, a priori atheism damaged the human person, forbidding him to be the desire for the gift and thus also to be a gift for others. Wojtyła called this prohibition an anthropological error. The communist *praxis* of a priori atheism safeguards the observance of this error with police tactics. The so-called Western world continues to safeguard this observance in a manner both rationalistic and irrational, and more sophisticated. What Soviet communism did not succeed in doing is now accomplished by Western bankers and politicians. Because Wojtyła saw the human person prophetically and poetically, he believed that anthropological error would end with the defeat of those who staked their lives on it. He was not only thinking of communism. Every separation of freedom from love cancels out the justice without which societies cannot live. The person is owed love and not the tolerance proclaimed by Enlightenment rationalism. Tolerance does not renounce violence. It offends the human person.

Man cannot live worthily or rightly without love. Plato already knew this. In Book II of *The Republic*, Glaucon proposes hypothetically that, "in our thoughts we grant to a just and an unjust person the freedom to do whatever they like. We can then follow both of them and see where their desires would lead. And we'll catch the just person red-handed travelling the same road as the unjust. The reason for this is the desire to outdo others and get more and more. This is what anyone's nature naturally pursues as good, but nature is forced by law into the perversion of treating fairness with respect. The freedom I mentioned would be most easily realized if both people had the power they say the ancestor of Gyges of Lydia possessed."[38]

---

37. Czesław Miłosz, "Oeconomia divina," in *New and Collected Poems 1931-2001* (New York: HarperCollins, 2001), p. 263.
38. Plato, *Republic* 2.359b-d.

Gyges served the king of Lydia as a shepherd. Once, during "a violent thunderstorm . . . an earthquake broke open the ground and created a chasm at the place where he was tending his sheep." Gyges entered the opening in the earth and saw things that astonished him. He saw a great bronze horse with doors. Upon looking inside, he discovered a giant corpse with a golden ring on its finger, which Gyges took and put on. After this he returned to his fellow shepherds. While speaking with them, he played with the ring on his finger. He realized that when he twisted the stone toward his palm, he became invisible to the other shepherds. *Technē* had destroyed his personal ties with others. Immediately, Gyges understood what power had fallen into his hands — and what possibility for obtaining more power. When the shepherds sent him to the king to give an account of their work, Gyges took the opportunity afforded to him by the ring. He made himself invisible, killed the king, married the queen, and took possession of the throne.

Technical "making," *facere* — this turn in the hand of the ring robbed from matter, submits people to an incomprehensible technical subject, to which they pass off their responsibility for what they have done. They no longer feel responsible because they do not dwell in their personal ties to other men: they have become invisible. By themselves, they do not create the greatest works of art. Rather, they do everything possible to acquire power, to which they submit themselves — so much so that they use themselves as instruments to attain it. They rob themselves of energy, that sacred fire toward which Prometheus sacrilegiously stretched out his hand. For God's transcendence they substitute what we might call the *transgressio* of one object by another. Wojtyła calls this *transgressio* horizontal transcendence. They arrogate to themselves the right to everything, above all the right not to be called by anyone. They do not want anyone to call them because they do not want to respond. They replace the *communio personarum* with what I would call *iuxtapositio*, the juxtaposition of visible objects in a calculated line. Since there is no place in that line for God's transcendence, there is also no place for the transcendence of man.

In this neat row of calculated objects, nothing is sacred (*sacrum*) but quantitative measurement, thanks to which some objects prevail over others. This is what I have just called *transgressio*. Calculating individuals know and accept only those differences that are economic or political in nature. Because they know no other differences, they sell even themselves *ad libitum*. They do not join themselves forever to another person,

Via pulchritudinis — via crucis

for calculation does not permit this. All that they are capable of doing can be reduced to counting money. For them, even love, beauty, and dignity are nothing more than a price tag.

It is unsettling. We do not notice that we are becoming a mass of Gyges who, hidden behind our technology, ambush and rob others like Prometheus, taking possession of the divine fire of energy that is in them and in the world. At times we use this fire to make things that are useful, but all too often we use it to overpower others. The modern Gyges moves blithely and blatantly through the world, without a care that Prometheus' destiny will also be his.

Society is not born in such people, for they are not visible to one another. They are interested only in the *technē* of twisting the ring on their finger, not in other people. Beauty does not captivate them. They don't see it or know how to receive it — and thus give themselves to it. Distancing themselves from the beautiful, they lose hope. They do not hear the "voice" of the Promise that calls them, and so they lose the prophet's vision of human life on earth. "Where there is no prophecy the people cast off restraint, but blessed is he who keeps the law" (Prov. 29:18). The law of love rules wherever vision prevails of the totality of all that is, wherever wonder prevails — wonder at the beauty of the true and the good that express themselves in the vision. "Vision is love's space," wrote Wojtyła.[39] I would add that it is also the space of faith and of hope, that is, the space of freedom. He who sees, loves and knows not only that which he sees. He knows also that which he does not see, but which leaves traces on the reality he contemplates, making it beautiful. These traces allow us not to remain blocked in this visible world. They lead us ever further, awakening in us a desire for him whose Beauty has left a reflection on beings accessible to human eyes.

> He who loves — wants to see at least the shadow of the figure,
> This is how we love Mother — Father — brothers —
> Our beloved — even God . . .
> He who loves, wants to see at least the shadow of the image
> At least a trace that leads to the beloved's bower,
> At least a pointing road sign,
> At least a cross, at least the invocation of a litany,

---

39. Karol Wojtyła, "Redemption Seeking Your Form to Enter Man's Anxiety: Name," in *Place Within*, p. 172.

> At least a tower of stone soaring
> Amid the lightning — to contemplate the face of God.[40]

The beautiful is difficult because the love that is revealed in it is difficult. We cannot take possession of it. We can only become it — which means that we must convert both to beauty and to love. Whoever converts, walks toward beauty and love and at the same time awaits them. This also means dying to that which is merely human. Plato holds that beauty in man is "divine reason ... within himself."[41] The Grand Inquisitor of Dostoyevsky's *The Brothers Karamazov* neither sees nor understands this beauty. He imprisons the One who in the beauty of his Person brings us the gift that liberates. If the Inquisitor allows him to live, it is only as one expelled from society, to whom every path of return has been barred. The kiss that Christ, the divine Poetry, places silently on the Inquisitor's lips troubles the man's heart, but his mind continues immovably in his calculated ideas. The Inquisitor justifies himself with these ideas, calling them philosophy so as the more easily to mislead people seeking an apparent happiness.[42]

The drama of modernity consists in the fact that the beautiful, which modernity has deformed, no longer defends man. It fragments him. Fortunately, however, it is impossible to overcome true beauty. Man can publicly reject it, but he cannot conquer it in his heart. He belongs to it even when he rejects it. In denying beauty, he denies himself. How long can one live in discord with oneself, that is, degrading the beauty that is the human person?

The beautiful opens the way to the Love that comes to us. It is the way to Love, the *via pulchritudinis* traced out not by the reasoning that Christ calls "flesh and blood" (cf. Matt. 16:17), but by itself, reflected in every being. Beauty is sheer gift. "If you knew the gift of God, and who it is that is saying to you, 'Give me a drink,' you would have asked him, and he would have given you living water" (John 4:10). Reason that avoids the beautiful, in which the person approaches another person, ceases to be

---

40. Cyprian Norwid, "Promethidion — Bogumił," in *Pisma wszystkie*, vol. 3, pp. 441-42.

41. Plato, *Republic* 590c-d.

42. Cf. St. Augustine, *Confessions* 3.4: "Sunt qui seducant per philosophiam magno et blando et honesto nomine colorantes et fucantes errors suos" ["There are people for whom philosophy is a means of misleading others, for they misuse its great name, its attractions, and its integrity to give color and gloss to their own errors."] Translation from St. Augustine, *Confessions*, trans. R. S. Pine-Coffin (New York: Penguin, 1961), p. 59.

reasonable. It does not know how to ask or to request, and therefore does not know how to think.

In order to "contemplate God's face," we must travel against the current of the "torrent of beauty" that flows through each human being. The source embraces us with the torrent.[43] We journey to the source continually bidding farewell to the beauty reflected in the torrent, which flows and passes on. We are compelled to bid farewell to every path, including the path that is the beautiful itself. Encounters with the beauty of the person, the fascination that this beauty has for us, and bidding farewell along the path that leads to the Source, form the history of faith in God and faith in man's unquiet heart. Man entrusts himself to God's Beauty by entrusting himself to its reflection in the "torrent of beauty" he encounters in the world. Precisely for this reason, the history of faith during the time in which this torrent flows is shaped by vigilance, petition, and prayer. These determine the rationality of human reason.

The desire for beauty, as well as vigilance so that it may not pass us by without our notice, form the essence of the poetry that is the person. Being person means to journey along the path of beauty toward the love whose "form" it is. Being person means to have a care adequately to confront this "form," even at the price of one's life.

> No! — what holds up the song is only reason,
> What is poured out in the psalm, only sorrow,
> What is grasped in the lyre-strings, only passion,
> What does not tremble with fear before the heart, firmness —
> Only reason, sorrow, passion and firmness
> Are worthy of history, because they have Hope,
> But all the rest — is error — is the tomb —
> Is worse than error and the tomb . . . is the whip!
> They will conquer the world . . . but never even a single note![44]

* * *

Love, flowing toward man in a "torrent of beauty," brings him the gift of a dignity infinitely greater than his humanity because it is the "trace" of

---

43. Cf. Karol Wojtyła, *Radiation of Fatherhood*, in *Collected Plays*, p. 351: "Through the stream the SOURCE EMBRACES ME TOO."

44. Cyprian Norwid, "Fulminant," in *Pisma wszystkie*, vol. 3, p. 545.

the divinity. The "torrent of beauty" promises us divinity. Bishop Wojtyła and then John Paul II spoke of this to artists.

When Karol Wojtyła spoke of moral experience, he referred to the original experience of beauty. It is upon this experience that he based his adequate anthropology. This anthropology is formed in the human person's dialogue with the Source of the "torrent of beauty." In this torrent, we hear the "voice" of the Source who calls us to himself with the "voice" of the true and the good. Metaphysics arises in the dialogue with this "voice." I think that precisely here, in the contemplation of the "torrent of beauty" that flows through the person who is present to other persons, Karol Wojtyła also found the link between phenomenology and metaphysics — the heart of which beats in those events that are the transcendentals *(ens, verum, bonum et pulchrum convertuntur)*.

Neither "pure" phenomenology nor "pure" academic metaphysics do justice to the human person if the first stops at the "pure" description of the "torrent"; or if the second, losing sight of the "torrent," stops at ideas constructed by reason *(ratio)*. Wojtyła avoids this danger. In dealing with the phenomenology of the person's original experience, he goes beyond simple description, grounding the metaphysical contemplation of being in the human person's moral experience. Always, in both phenomenological description and metaphysical contemplation, he looks at the human person from a viewpoint that is above him.

In the space of the beauty of persons who are present to one another, communion between them is born. Each person is reborn in the beauty of the other. In the dialogue that takes place in the "torrent of beauty," they reverence the truth that the torrent reveals and kneel before its Source. Their astonishment at the beauty that passes is the beginning of their adoration of the Beauty that is eternity. The individual who remains outside of the dialogue in which the communion of persons arises can describe what appears to him, but he cannot perceive the truth. The truth reveals itself in persons who are present to others. Outside of the communion of persons, "first philosophy," or metaphysics, is impossible. And without metaphysics, phenomenological description builds castles in the sand. The return to the Source of the "torrent of beauty" restores life to the person and to his philosophical thinking, binding him to the true and the good that the "torrent" has brought to him.

Karol Wojtyła was altogether predestined to unite the phenomenological description of the human person's act with its metaphysical substrate *(suppositum)*. Beyond being rooted in the experience of mystics, he belonged to a people educated not by philosophers enslaved by the *cogito* and crushed by its constructions, but by poets and thinkers who were inspired by their experience of the "torrent of beauty." Norwid, who is one of the greatest Polish poets — if not the greatest — brilliantly expressed moral experience in the poem "Promethidion," from which Wojtyła and later Pope John Paul II drew inspiration.

> Beauty is the form of love . . .
> Because a lamp cannot remain under a bushel basket,
> Nor the salt of the earth among the kitchen spices.
> Beauty is to make you eager to work —
> And work is for man to gain his resurrection.[45]

John Paul II lived poetically during the years of his pontificate. But only at the end of his life did he return to the "great lady," as he called poetry. He reproached himself for not having always remained faithful to her. In *Roman Triptych*, he immersed himself once again in the "torrent of beauty," to help us join him in contemplating his own Petrine ministry in the Church. This time the question, "Source, where are you?" was asked in the Sistine Chapel, before Michelangelo's *Last Judgment*. Wonder at the Source that is Love was united with the trembling that comes in the face of the End, which is also Love. John Paul II contemplated this work with eyes that are not "kept from recognizing" (cf. Luke 24:16) by the aesthetic of pure forms. In this work, he sought the Love that asked him three times, "Do you love me?"

At the end of his life, Love revealed to John Paul II a new meaning of the words that had been spoken to him during the days of the conclave by the man who had been his rector, Cardinal Maximilian de Fürstenberg: *"Magister adest et vocat te"* ["The Teacher is here and is calling you"]. Even in the very last stage of his life, John Paul II thought above all of the Church, who will seek the Source of the "torrent of beauty" beneath the Last Judgment until the end of the world. God's Beauty, which shines forth in Christ, also embraces and unites us in him. The Beauty that Pilate indicates with the words, *"Ecce homo!"* — "Behold, the man!" — enraptures us. In its light, we see what we have done to the truth of our being and so judge ourselves. At the same time, Beauty itself judges us through

---

45. Cyprian Norwid, "Promethidion," in *Pisma wszystkie*, vol. 3, pp. 437, 439-40.

us, but differently than we do. We are not beauty, for it merely flows through us: "Such Beauty is called Mercy."[46]

Everything that John Paul II said about the human person can be summarized in the question regarding love and work (cf. Gen. 1:28). The story of their unity is interwoven with the story of man, the story of humanity and the story of the Church. This story must have been a difficult drama for Blessed John Paul II. In the first years of his pontificate he confided to someone, "Only death will free me from this cross!" But he was not alone. He was saved by the moral experience of the beautiful in people who were present to him. Together with them, he contemplated the human person and the starry heaven. Together with them, he listened to the "voice" of his and their moral conscience. With the help of prayer, he "completed the definition" of his own being.[47] He passed like passing time, but at the same time became himself. He died to be born. For him, the End was the Beginning. Because he was disinterested, he was a free man. At the beginning of the Petrine ministry, he was condemned to death "for your and our freedom."[48] He had been laboriously conquering this freedom for himself and for others in Krakow and Rome, so he knew very well what he was saying when he wrote,

> Freedom has continually to be won, it cannot merely be possessed. It comes as a gift but can only be kept with a struggle. Gift and struggle are written into pages, hidden yet open.
>
> You pay for freedom with all your being, therefore call this your freedom, that paying for it continually you possess yourself anew.[49]

The beauty of the person is very difficult. Man reveals it by carrying it on his own cross until the moment when, like a grain of wheat, he is cast into the earth to be reborn in it.

The beauty of the person who is beaten, wounded, and bleeding — but who resists in freedom — moves and fascinates us, and provokes our

---

46. Wojtyła, *Our God's Brother*, p. 227 (translation slightly altered).

47. I have borrowed this term from Roman Ingarden. According to Ingarden, every work of art demands of the one contemplating it a *dookreślenie*, that is, the completion of its definition. This is the co-creation of the work of art together with the artist, who in everything that he *did* express, did not express it to the end.

48. The Polish independence fighters of the nineteenth century wrote these words on their flags.

49. Karol Wojtyła, "Thinking My Country: I Reach the Heart of the Drama," in *Place Within*, p. 145.

compassion. The beauty of the weary person at Jacob's well asks, "Give me a drink" (John 4:7). The beauty of the person nailed to the cross cries out, "I thirst!" (John 19:28). This is how John Paul II desired the friendly presence of others. The desire for the presence of others gave form to his priestly service. He sought out their presence daily.

A few conversations with him have remained imprinted in my memory. They allowed me the better to understand the parable of the prodigal son, in which the father rejoices at his younger son's return to the beautiful truth of the family home, while he is saddened by the elder son's destiny. The elder son, caught up in lies, acts for the sake of his "career," waiting for the day when his father's property will become his possession. Like the father in the parable, John Paul II, a priest who was totally and disinterestedly open to others, was saddened by the careerism he at times saw all around him.

The beauty of the work of art that is the human person profoundly moves whoever contemplates it. This beauty provokes tremors in the deepest strata of our being. Like a light breath of wind, it opens new pages in the book of our life. It helps us discover new spaces in ourselves, the definition of which still needs completion. We did not remember these spaces while, hidden in our interior, they awaited our love and work. But the "eternal man" does not forget them. It is to him that we must pose our question about beauty, since he "is not envious . . . and waits without covetousness" (Norwid). What the "eternal man" knows best is love, the beautiful, and work. From him, we learn that the beauty that reveals itself in the true and the good is the "form of love" — the form that calls us to work for the true and the good that do not pass away.

Beauty proclaims the Future to us; it proclaims a new world that already shines through love and work. Beauty proclaims to man his new birth. There are, however, no births without suffering. The beautiful enraptures, but it also provokes suffering.

> Eternal future! Be for me from afar
> A dawn shining beyond the abyss;
> But until I have reached the third heaven,
> Be for me only like God's grace,
> For I must still hew my cross in the world
> Before it is placed in my dead hands![50]

50. Cyprian Norwid, "W Pamiętniku L. A. — Improwizacja," in *Pisma wszystkie*, vol. 1, p. 74.

John Paul II showed — or perhaps merely reminded us — that it is impossible to distinguish the *via pulchritudinis* from the *via crucis*. The true and the good "happen" only on this beautiful but sorrowful path; we attain freedom with these transcendentals only on this path. The *via dolorosa pulchritudinis* [the sorrowful way of beauty] leads to the Love that is the "Father of great poetry," that is, the Father of immense, paschal freedom.

Every person walks a path to beauty that is destined for him alone. Beauty has many names. It does not repeat itself. With a polyphony made up of an infinity of voices, it speaks of the very reality that is beyond words, sound, and colors. Beauty is free of these, even though it reveals itself in them and tells of itself with their aid. It leads those who entrust themselves to it beyond the visibility of the world's forms — and even of their very being. The way of the beautiful is a paschal way, upon which even God journeyed when he became man.

The beauty of the human body, the beauty of human thoughts and actions, the beauty of the work of art, the beauty of the universe is a paschal beauty. On the way of beauty, we must constantly bid farewell, for we may not stop on any part of the path. We must give ourselves not to the way, but to him to whom the way leads, for we belong to him. The way of the beautiful "on this field that is not eternal" leads to the Beauty of the "eternal Future."[51]

The beautiful is difficult, but this does not mean that we should flee from it. Christ's words, so often repeated by John Paul II, "Be not afraid!," free us not only from fear in the face of inhuman systems, but also from the fear with which people often approach their body, their thoughts, and actions. They forget that God's merciful Beauty transcends their moral conscience. Lowering our eyes at the sight of a beautiful body breaks off the path to knowing the truth that begins to reveal itself in that body. We have only to remember that the beautiful is not an object to be conquered or possessed. We must *become* it, and this happens only on the *via crucis* — because beauty is paschal. Man should be ashamed of himself when he looks at his own body and at the body of the other person as if they were objects to be used and then thrown onto the scrap-heap.

Betrayal of the beautiful eliminates not only its paschal character, but the paschal character of the human person. Beauty, on the other hand, does not betray man. This is why it is called mercy. Mercy cannot be de-

---

51. Cf. Norwid, "W Pamiętniku L. A. — Improwizacja," in *Pisma wszystkie*, vol. 1, p. 73.

feated. It can be crucified, but the crucifixion does not mean the victory of those who nail it to the cross. Merciful beauty is victor on the cross.

> Oh! art — rainbow of the eternal Jerusalem,
> You are the bow of the Covenant — after the floods
> Of history.[52]

* * *

Bishop Karol Wojtyła became aware of the human person by meditating philosophically on the beautiful act in which the person reveals himself.[53] In such an act, the person is reborn in the truth, which is present in the love that unites persons into one. Wojtyła contemplated the beauty of their communion, in the Spirit of the beauty of the divine and human love that blows "where it wills, and you hear the sound of it, but you do not know whence it comes or where it is going" (John 3:8). In doing so, Wojtyła drew near to the truth of man conceived and fulfilled by God, in the beauty of communion with his merciful Word.

Beauty unveils itself in man in such a way that he must still seek it in order to be beautiful himself. He must ask for it and ask questions about it. In the spiritual exercises for artists we mentioned above,[54] Bishop Wojtyła continually repeated that the artist's work of creating, which takes place within the flowing "torrent of beauty," is owed to the Source. If an artist is truly an artist, he creates works of art — especially the work of art that he himself is — with wonder and a sense of gratitude, crying uninterruptedly, "Where are you? . . . Source, where are you?!"[55] Ingratitude degenerates into an idolatry of one's own feelings, impressions, and talent. The work of an artist caught in such idolatry shatters into fragments, saying nothing. A work of art that does not speak with a vision of the whole and with silence (which is the language of this vision) cannot be a space in which the human person enters into friendship with a wisdom greater than himself. In his poem, "Words' Resistance to Thought," Wojtyła writes of the human person,

---

52. Cyprian Norwid, "Promethidion — Wstęp," in *Pisma wszystkie*, vol. 3, pp. 427-28.
53. Cf. Karol Wojtyła, *Person and Act*. See note 2 of chap. 1.
54. Wojtyła, *Ewangelia a sztuka*.
55. John Paul II, *The Poetry of John Paul II: Roman Triptych*, trans. Jerzy Peterkiewicz (Washington, DC: USCCB, 2003), p. 9.

> If he suffers, deprived of vision,
> he must tear through the thicket of signs
> to the word's very center,
> its weight the ripeness of fruit.[56]

"Tearing through the thicket of signs" in suffering means maturing toward vision — and toward the ultimate word that is silence.

After the Polish poet Czesław Miłosz received the Nobel Prize for Literature, John Paul II received him in a private audience. During the conversation, which I witnessed, the Pope asked him about his plans for the future. "At my age," the poet replied, "it's hard to make plans. The best thing I could do would be to translate the Bible." On April 2, 2004, four months prior to his death, Miłosz sent a letter to the Pope with the request, "Holy Father, age changes perspectives. When I was young, a poet's request for a papal blessing would have been thought inopportune. But this is precisely my preoccupation, since in the last few years I have been careful not to distance myself from Catholic orthodoxy while writing poetry, and I do not know whether I have succeeded. So I ask of you a word that confirms my tending toward the goal that we share. May Christ's promise on the day of his Resurrection be accomplished." The Pope wrote him a reply:

> Dear Sir, I read your letter of April 2 with great emotion — or rather, I read it several times. Its few words contain a rich and varied content. You write that the object of your preoccupation has been "not to distance yourself from Catholic orthodoxy" in your poetical work. I am convinced that such an attitude on the part of the Poet is decisive. In this sense, I am glad to be able to confirm your words regarding your "tending toward the goal that we share." I wish with all my heart that in each of us — in your life and in mine — the greatest promise that Christ made to mankind in his Resurrection may be accomplished. I wish you in your life and in the creation of works of art the blessing of God.[57]

The man who does not perceive signs or, worse, opposes them, closes himself up in his own univocal immanence. Deprived of their apophatic

---

56. John Paul II, "Thought — Strange Space: Words' Resistance to Thought," in *Place Within*, p. 55.

57. I cite following Andrzej Franaszek, *Miłosz: Biografia* (Krakow: Wydawn. Znak, 2011), pp. 742-43.

help, he will not be able to open the path that leads him through himself. For this reason, he will not enter into "that which lies within" his person. Even when he does notice signs, he needs an artist greater than himself who can help him perceive that to which they point. He needs the "Father of great poetry," who tells him what poetry is and explains to him how one becomes a poet, that is, a human being. Paraphrasing Nietzsche, we can say that man needs a Savior much more than he needs ethical geniuses.

The wonder prompted by the "torrent of beauty" that points to its Source creates the space in which man sees and judges himself in the light of the Transcendence of the Origin and End. If, looking at himself in the light of the End, he can say, "You are more beautiful now than you were!," it will be only thanks to the Mercy of Beauty.

Wonder at the Origin and concern for what will become of this wonder at the End permeated Wojtyła in the Polish landscape and matured in his "pilgrimage to the holy places," the places "of human flourishing"[58] — that is, places where man loves and works most. Any place can be holy because, through love and work, every place can be Mount Horeb and Golgotha. Anywhere that man can be aflame like the burning bush or set his own cross in the earth is holy. In other words, man can find his own country anywhere.

Karol Wojtyła matured under the cross he took up as he followed Christ. Under this cross, he learned to suffer. In other words, he learned to receive the true and the good that was traced out in the Origin, but only brought to completion in the End by the merciful Beauty that was "exhausted" for our sake.[59] Only Mercy can bring the metaphysics of human love to fulfillment, by fulfilling the truth and the goodness revealed in it. Only Mercy can bring metaphysics to fulfillment. To Adam Chmielowski — the future Brother Albert — who asked on what path he might receive the grace of purification, his confessor gives only one piece of advice: "Let yourself be molded by love."[60]

In the last few days of his life, John Paul II's person shone with the beautiful. The invisible light emanating from his agony made the visible world more legible and comprehensible to those who were spiritually

---

58. Cf. Karol Wojtyła, *Pellegrinaggio ai luoghi santi*, in *Opere letterarie* (Vatican City: Libreria Editrice Vaticana, 1993), pp. 122 and 126.

59. Cf. Wojtyła, *Our God's Brother*, p. 227.

60. Wojtyła, *Our God's Brother*, p. 210.

present to him. They saw that the path that leads from time to eternity passes through the love nailed to the cross.

The witness *(martyrion)* that man bears to God under the cross "completes" the commandments *(martyria)* that God has written in human hearts as a witness to his love. God has made the human heart an Ark of the Testimony and of his Covenant with man (cf. Exod. 25:16). The *martyria* of God judge the *martyrion* of man: the Love that is God judges the love that man has become in response to it. No testimony can be generalized. God offers the *martyria* of his Love to each person, and each of us exists oriented toward God as a single, unrepeatable response: *martyrion*.

The moral experience that takes place precisely in this dialogue of witnesses shows us that man's welcoming God and belonging to God exclude all arbitrary will. The moral experience takes place in the mystical sphere of human life. Man exists as a personal subject in union with the other, whose beauty fascinates him to the point that he can say, "You are mine and I am yours!" There is no place for such a confession in the subject-object relation. That relation is dominated by the "master-slave" dialectic, in which the word "mine" — the word the "master" uses for the "servant" and the "servant" for the "master" — means something completely different. A rational freedom reigns only in the dialogue of witnesses, which unites persons into one.

Under Christ's cross, man looks at himself with a rational tranquility. His work, ordered by Beauty crucified "here" and by the "great question," creates a culture of acts and words oriented to God the "Father of great poetry" rather than to circumstances. The Beauty the Father pronounced in eternity and we crucified in time "en-humans" itself *(en-anthropesen)*[61] in a specific historical moment and geographical place. He does this so that man might not lose himself in infinite time and space, or be disheartened by their eternal silence.[62]

> God has come as far as that,
> stopped but a step from nothingness,
> so near our eyes.
> It seemed to simple hearts,

---

61. For the Greek term from which I adapt this neologism, cf. St. Athanasius of Alexandria, *O wcieleniu Słowa* [*De incarnatione Verbi*] (Warsaw: Akademia Teologii Katolickiej, 1998), p. 73.

62. Cf. Blaise Pascal, *Pensées*, no. 91.

Via pulchritudinis — via crucis

to open hearts it seemed
that He was lost amidst the ears of corn.[63]

He disappeared, lost amid the ears of grain transfigured in the Eucharist. Man asks his fundamental question to the Word of God, who stopped "but a step from nothingness" — the question about the meaning of life created in this "nothingness." This Word "lost amidst the ears of corn" is, as Hölderlin says, the "Spirit of today":

Much I said to him; for whatever the poets may ponder,
Sing, it mostly concerns either the angels or Him.[64]

With Hölderlin's words, the first two sentences of the encyclical *Redemptor hominis* come together: "The Redeemer of man, Jesus Christ, is the center of the universe and of history. To him go my thoughts and my heart in this solemn moment of the world that the Church and the whole family of present-day humanity are now living."

Mysticism and poetry prepared Karol Wojtyła to face the prose that postmodernity constructed in a forgetfulness of the Beauty that saves — and consequently in a forgetfulness of the truth and the good of the human person. Poetry showed Wojtyła the beautiful present *in fieri* in the human person. Mysticism governed his metaphysical thought, focusing it on man's contingent *esse*, his being. This *esse* owes much to human beings, but everything to God. Man marvels not so much at the sight of his own being *(esse)* as at that which comes to be in its "shadow" *(fieri)*. What comes to be is true reality.

I bring you good news of great wonder, Hellenic masters:
it is pointless to watch over existence
which slips out of our hands,
for there is a Beauty more real
concealed in the living blood.

A morsel of bread is more real
than the universe.[65]

63. Karol Wojtyła, "Song of the Hidden God: Shores of Silence," in *Place Within*, p. 10.
64. Friedrich Hölderlin, "Homecoming: To His Relatives," in *Poems and Fragments*, p. 333.
65. Karol Wojtyła, "Song of the Hidden God," p. 11.

Karol Wojtyła's philosophy was identical with dialogue — the dialogue of his *martyrion* with the *martyrion* of others, and the dialogue of their communal *martyrion* with the *martyria* of God. He made use of the phenomenological method to describe the human person's beautiful becoming (*fieri*) in these dialogues. Immersed in the "torrent of beauty," he listened metaphysically to the "voices" of his *esse*, his being. That is, he listened to the transcendentals of the true and the good. Whoever does not know what mysticism and poetry are will not understand the metaphysics of the mystery of the person. He will not understand the incomprehensible work of art that is love in the human person. Such a metaphysics takes place beyond every description. This event, which cannot be comprehended on earth, is the content of Karol Wojtyła's adequate anthropology.

* * *

The priest Karol Wojtyła elevated his pastoral interaction with young people to the sphere of a shared contemplation of God's Beauty, which flows through every human being. The insidious hands of the police who carried out the orders of their communist henchmen, convinced that the ideology they imposed was the salvation of man, did not reach so high. For the young people to whom Wojtyła ministered and for their spiritual guide, these pastoral groups, governed by duties and rights rediscovered in the love that united people, formed a kind of mountaintop refuge. On these heights forgotten by postmodernity, it was clear that the person is saved by the presence of the other person. The communist henchmen lived like parasites atop isolated persons. In isolation, we cannot see the truth that liberates only those who live in communion. The actions of isolated persons are a-logical, so much so that they cannot but surrender to the logic of nihilistic reasoning and to the foolish, servile arguments of the power that seeks to beat people into such reasoning.

I do not recall specific conversations with Bishop Wojtyła or with Pope John Paul II about postmodernity. In Krakow, only Sartre worried him, because of the iron logic with which the French philosopher drew the consequences of the denial of God's existence. At the time, we were dealing with an atheistic trampling of the dignity of the human person by means of the secret police. This violation of the person already implied the negation of God. Our experience of the trampling of human dignity was enough for us to know what the denial of God was and could be. One does not dialogue with the trampling of the human person; the intellectuals of the West did not understand this. We had the advantage of being able to bear witness to what we had seen, whereas they bore witness only to their argumentation.

Out of necessity, we focused on the Love that was made flesh and dwelt among us: this is where we sought refuge. Our questions about him contained a remembering of the commandment that rang out in Paradise: "Do not speak to the 'serpent'!" The men of the West, often men of the Church, did not understand us. They reproached us for not knowing how to dialogue with . . . the serpent. They spoke of diplomacy, of an academic dialogue. We, on the other hand, were compelled to get by with the serpent's communist administration. We had to survive without denying our moral conscience. So we did not pay any attention to the criticisms of the West. When it was necessary and possible, we told how things were without a lot of plays on words, but we often used the cover of a metaphorical language offered by myths or historical events, such as the conflict between Antigone and Creon or St. Stanislas and King Boleslas.

Bishop Wojtyła saw many people paralyzed by fear along the way toward the true and the good. This is why he repeated Christ's words so firmly, "Do not be afraid!" I was once summoned for an interrogation by the secret police. The Bishop, saying goodbye to me at the door of his apartment, clasped my hand very tightly and spoke these few but powerful words: "Don't be afraid! *Dabitur tibi in illa hora!* ['It will be given to you in that hour what you are to say']." And that's what happened. People cease to be afraid when they keep watch and pray together. The moral conscience defends their freedom.

> History lays down events over the struggles of conscience. Victories throb inside this layer, and defeats. History does not cover them: it makes them stand out.
> Can history ever flow against the current of conscience? . . .
> Weak is a people that accepts defeat, forgetting that it was sent to keep watch till the coming of its hour. And the hours keep returning on the great clockface of history.
> This, the liturgy of history. Vigil is the word of the Lord and the word of the People, which we continually receive anew.[66]

---

66. Karol Wojtyła, "Thinking My Country: Thinking My Country I Return to the Tree," in *Place Within*, pp. 148-49.

A people is strong when it keeps watch and awaits the dawn of the truth of man. Only such a people will not betray itself, because only such a people is not afraid to speak the word with which it was sent to others. The way of this people is the *via pulchritudinis et crucis*, the way of beauty and the cross.

CHAPTER 3

The New Evangelization

The human person doesn't *need* evangelization. He *desires* it. We don't *need* God, we *desire* him. We "need" to possess something more than we already possess, but we desire to be greater — to be other than we are now. Only God is greater than man. Our desire to become God allows us and in some measure obliges us to live in a paschal way. The human person is himself only when he bids farewell to the road he is traveling — to everything in the world and in himself that passes away — and unites himself to that which remains. He is himself when he tends toward and nurtures that which remains in him. What remains is the meaning of what passes away. As Norwid says, in man, everything but beauty and goodness passes away. These two things do not pass away because their Source, God, does not pass away. The restless human heart speaks of God, and the desire of this restless heart creates poetry and goodness.

In its essence, evangelization is always the same because neither God, the Lord of time, nor the desire of man's restless heart is subject to change. Only the circumstances change in which the human person asks about God and seeks him. Doubtless these circumstances influence the human heart. They can even suffocate its voice to the extent that it no longer resembles a heart but rather a hardened mass, the "hardness of heart" *(sklerokardia)* of which Christ speaks in the Gospel of Matthew (cf. Matt. 19:8). But changing circumstances never have so much influence that they force the heart to cease to be itself. In other words, they never force it to stop taking its orientation from its restlessness for God.

The circumstances that together form postmodernity favor man's dialogue with the "serpent." Our contemporaries base themselves on the serpent's poisonous questions and on the answers these questions already contain. Detached from the Origin, which is the act of creation, and the End, which is the fulfillment of what was created, they seek to construct their own homes. They do not build on the foundation of the truth present in poetry and goodness, but on changing opinions. Influenced by the latter, they dream of possessing what makes life simultaneously comfortable and unworthy of man. Comfort, treated as if it were the truth sought by man's restless heart, divides people into conflicting parties and cliques. Postmodernity violates the person; it forces him to dwell in comfortable negations of the truth. Since postmodern reason has been uprooted from man's restless heart and from Him whom this heart desires, this reason entrusts itself only to itself. It does not enter into a personal dialogue with other people or God. A reason rooted only in itself reduces everything, the human person included, to a commodity with a quantifiable price.

So we must not identify the new evangelization, which we hear about more and more today, with thinking up new apostolic projects. Evangelization will always consist, on the one hand, in leading the person out of a dialogue with the "serpent" and hope in his promises; and on the other hand, with the incessant search for the path to God — a search announced by the restless heart in every human being. Christ's words are forever relevant: "Convert and believe in the Gospel!" (Mark 1:15). Every morning we have to come out of the world of dreams and begin a new life in the world. Reality, continually created anew, is waiting for us there. In the world of dreams, we live in solitude, in which there is no place for evangelization.

There is no other evangelization than the one inscribed in the human person who, because he desires to remain himself, desires to be evangelized. In order to be himself, man must change his life, entrusting himself to the One who is greater than he and to whom he belongs. The prophets began to "read" the human person and to admonish him. Reading and admonishing man, John the Baptist "proclaimed a baptism of conversion" (Mark 1:4). He announced the coming of one "mightier" than he, who would baptize "in the Holy Spirit" (Matt. 3:11). The Baptist pointed out the Way on which the human person must set out if he wants to walk toward God. In the Holy Spirit, this Way leads through death.

In order the better to understand what this phrase, the "new evangelization," means, we must recall its origins.

The idea of the new evangelization arose in Bishop Karol Wojtyła in the course of his struggle for the visible presence of the cross in the life of Polish society. Pope John Paul II first spoke of a "new evangelization" under the cross of the Cistercian Abbey at Mogiła, near Krakow, not far from Nowa Huta, where people struggled against the Communist police in defense of the cross erected on their land:

> Let us go together, pilgrims, to the Lord's Cross. With it begins a new era in human history. This is the time of grace, the time of salvation. *Through the Cross man has been able to understand the meaning of his own destiny, of his life on earth.* ...
>
> ... *The history of Nowa Huta is also written* by means of the Cross. ...
>
> Where the Cross is raised, there is raised the sign that that place has now been reached by the Good News of Man's salvation through Love. Where the cross is raised, *there is the sign that evangelization has begun.* Once our fathers raised the Cross in various places in the land of Poland as a sign that the Gospel had arrived there, that there had been a beginning of the evangelization that was to continue without break until today.[1]

When at Nowa Huta a cross was raised for which people had to struggle, and in defense of which some of them died,

> we were given *a sign* that on the threshold of the new millennium, in these new times, these new conditions of life, the Gospel is again being proclaimed. *A new evangelization* has begun, as if it were a new proclamation, even if in reality it is the same as ever. The Cross stands high over the revolving world.
>
> Today, before the Cross of Mogiła, the Cross of Nowa Huta, let us give thanks for the new beginning of evangelization that has been brought about here. And let us all pray that it may be as fruitful as the first evangelization — indeed, even more fruitful.[2]

Under the cross of Nowa Huta, where the Ark Church was built and consecrated by Cardinal Wojtyła in 1977, a new people was born. "The new cross ... proclaimed *the birth of the new church*. This birth is deeply

---

1. John Paul II, homily for Holy Mass at the Shrine of the Holy Cross, Mogiła, June 9, 1979, no. 1. Given during John Paul II's first papal visit to Poland.

2. John Paul II, homily for Holy Mass, no. 1.

engraved on my heart and, when I left the see of Saint Stanislaus for the see of Saint Peter, I took it with me as a new relic, a priceless relic of our time." Under this cross, people were transformed. Their work was transformed, because under this cross, their love matured to the resurrection. The mystery of love, of work, and of the resurrection is bound to the mystery of the cross. "The Cross cannot be separated from man's work. Christ cannot be separated from man's work. This has been confirmed here at Nowa Huta. This has been the start of the new evangelization at the beginning of the new millennium of Christianity in Poland. We have lived this new beginning together and I took it with me *from Krakow to Rome as a relic*."[3] Recalling the places where he had worked as a laborer, he said, "Through all these surroundings, through his own experience of work, I make bold to say that the Pope *learned the Gospel anew*."[4] "From the cross of Nowa Huta began the new evangelization, *the evangelization of the second Millennium*."[5] In the life of the Church in Poland, Providence linked this new evangelization to the teaching of the Second Vatican Council.

The gospel is not proclaimed by functionaries who organize symposia and conferences. It is proclaimed by people who stand under the cross, convert to God, and so bear witness to Truth and Love crucified. They bear witness to the Event indicated by the empty tomb. In their care for holiness of life, wisdom is realized — which does not have much to do with the erudition of the learned. Words that have no effect in man negate evangelization. As Norwid writes,

> Those who were attentive made an effort for a day, the strong for a century.
> But the learned, as usual, formed a committee.[6]

As John Paul II told us, only those who are "attentive" and "strong" recognize their own divine and human humanity. They recognize this not with impersonal reasoning but with their lives, lived paschally. Theology and anthropology are not created by members of committees, but by witnesses to a paschal humanity that is oriented to God. Witnesses are

---

3. John Paul II, homily for Holy Mass, no. 2.
4. John Paul II, homily for Holy Mass, no. 2.
5. John Paul II, homily for Holy Mass, no. 3.
6. Cyprian Norwid, "Epimenides. Przypowieść," in *Pisma wszystkie*, vol. 3 (Warsaw: Państwowy Instytut Wydawniczy, 1971), p. 61.

martyrs.[7] Slaves ridicule and criticize the witnesses of Truth nailed to the cross. Sometimes they even kill the witnesses. The prophets were very aware of this, but so were men of Plato's stamp.

The new evangelization of Europe and of the world needs the theology and anthropology of martyr-witnesses. It is they who labor for the growth of the glory of God that is man, while empty erudition causes a commotion and then passes away. "Over the centuries in the West and the East the power of the Church has lain in the witness of the *saints*, of those who made Christ's truth their own truth, who followed the way that is Christ Himself and who lived the life that flows from Him in the Holy Spirit. And in the Eastern and Western Churches these saints have never been lacking."[8]

Holy men and women do not allow themselves to be caught up in sterile gossip and other similarly sterile actions. They wrestle with God until the dawn to obtain a blessing for themselves and for others, so that they can face the ever new challenges that a changing world presents to the Church. The new evangelization has to do not with a mechanical restoration or with proselytism,[9] but with the holiness of Christians. In other words, it has to do with their return to the cross, next to which they discover the empty tomb. Human persons are not to be reformed; rather, they are reborn. Reforms of the person always come too late.

Without the *scientia crucis* of people who stand under the cross, society becomes a mass of individuals who may at times function intelligently, but who always act stupidly, because they lack the meaning to which the empty tomb points. They debase themselves in their hiding places, where they seek a refuge that allows them to escape the cross. This anthropological error, which consists in refusing to be *martyrion*, makes them fall prey to the conviction that life is exhausted here and now, *in saeculo*. Hiding, that is, fleeing from the cross and the empty tomb, they become secularized.

Returning from the hospital, where he had an artificial hip joint implanted after breaking his leg, John Paul II said at the Angelus of May 29, 1994, "I understood that I had to introduce Christ's Church into the third millennium with prayer and with various initiatives, but I saw that these

---

7. The Greek word *martyr* means "witness."

8. John Paul II, *Crossing the Threshold of Hope*, trans. Jenny McPhee and Martha McPhee (New York: Knopf, 1994), p. 176.

9. Cf. John Paul II, *Crossing the Threshold of Hope*, p. 115.

are not enough. I had to introduce it with suffering, with the assassination attempt of thirteen years ago and with this new sacrifice. . . . The Pope had to be attacked, the Pope had to suffer so that every family in the world might see that there is, so to speak, a higher gospel: the gospel of suffering, with which we have to prepare the future, the third millennium." John Paul II carried his cross to the last breath of his life. At the beginning of his pontificate, he said to one of his friends, "Only death will free me from the cross I carry." Each of us carries his own cross to the last moment when, with the ultimate act of his person — that is, death — and with God's help, he begins a new life.

The human person will not have the courage to come forth from his hiding place if he does not allow himself to be enraptured by the Beauty of Truth and Love nailed to the cross. For people not enraptured by this Beauty, the cross is a wall and standing beneath it is meaningless. But for those who are enraptured, it is the door that leads to the Transcendence that fulfills the human being. "Suffering seems to belong to man's transcendence: it is one of those points in which man is in a certain sense 'destined' to go beyond himself, and he is called to this in a mysterious way."[10] In a world of the technical multiplication of commodities and pleasures, teaching people to accept that they are "destined" to the happiness we glimpse in the sacrifice of the cross is not easy. It can be accomplished only by those who have glimpsed in this "destiny" the truth of their own humanity, and have allowed themselves to be enraptured by its difficult beauty. On June 10, 1999, at Siedlce, Poland, John Paul II said, "The new evangelization needs true witnesses of faith. It needs people rooted in the Cross of Christ and ready to accept sacrifice for the sake of the Cross. Authentic witness to the life-giving power of the Cross is given by those who, in its name, overcome in themselves sin, egoism and every evil, and want to imitate the love of Christ to the very end."[11]

When John Paul II was asked what single sentence he would save out of the whole Bible if the latter had to be destroyed, he answered, "The truth will set you free." This response arose from his experience that the Church hides itself when she does not lead man to the Truth that suffers on the cross and rises again. She ceases to be Church. John Paul II knew from experience that we are not sustained on our journey to the cross

---

10. John Paul II, *Salvifici doloris*, apostolic letter on the Christian meaning of human suffering, February 11, 1984, no. 2.

11. John Paul II, homily for Eucharistic celebration at Siedlce, June 10, 1999, no. 4.

The New Evangelization

with argumentation, however sophisticated. Arguments do not introduce us into the country of Transcendence. Transcendence is always new, whereas arguments are always old. God's Transcendence, as well as the transcendence of the human person, calls us to go ever further — further than thought can reach. A little further on, there is only the cross and the resurrection. A little further on, the "first and last things" open up; witnesses to the cross begin to live them anew every day. They are reborn. The human person, who is destined for rebirth, is not permitted to stop even with the angels.

We think logically only under the cross. Only there, once we have become the "great question" to which God alone is the answer, can we think adequately of the Transcendence of God and the transcendence of our own person. From there, we think coherently with the Past and the Future, which are greater than anything that can be conceived. This is why crucified Love cannot be eliminated from human affairs. The Spirit of crucified Love renews man and the earth. The Spirit of crucified Love evangelizes! In Warsaw on June 2, 1979, John Paul II laid down this challenge to the Spirit of Love: "And I cry — I who am a son of the land of Poland and who am also Pope John Paul II — I cry from all the depths of this Millennium, I cry on the vigil of Pentecost: Let your Spirit descend. Let your Spirit descend and renew the face of the earth, the face of this land!" When he uttered this cry, the Communist darkness that covered Poland began to disperse, giving way to the morning of a new day. The gift of freedom showed itself to be a great task, which conferred the right to be oneself. On that Pentecost Sunday of 1979, the new evangelization came into being.

In the course of the same pilgrimage to Poland, in Krakow, John Paul II asked this question in faith to the Polish people and to all of mankind:

> Can one cast all this off? Can one say no? Can one refuse Christ and all that he has brought into human history?
>
> Certainly not. It is true that man is free. But the basic question remains: is it licit to do this?[12]

I remind you that in the years 1989-91, during which the inhuman Communist system was collapsing in Central and Eastern Europe, including in the Soviet Union, John Paul II was giving his catecheses on the Holy Spirit.

---

12. John Paul II, homily for Holy Mass in honor of St. Stanislaus, Krakow, June 10, 1979, no. 2.

From under the cross, we move toward our fellow men to tell them what is happening in our life. Under the cross is the Person of the living God, who "happens" in man. St. Paul, overcome suddenly by a "light from heaven" on the road to Damascus, fell to the ground and heard the call, "Preach the word, be urgent in season and out of season, convince, rebuke, and exhort, be unfailing in patience and in teaching" (2 Tim. 4:2).

The "light from heaven" not only shows us signs, but teaches us how to understand them. Merely seeing is not enough. Nicodemus begins his dialogue with Jesus by exhibiting his knowledge: "Rabbi, we know that you are a teacher come from God; for no one can do these signs that you do, unless God is with him" (John 3:2). Jesus, seeing that the difficulty for Nicodemus was not so much understanding the signs as entrusting himself to their Author, calls his attention to the love in which the person is born: "Truly, truly, I say to you, unless one is born of water and the Spirit, he cannot enter the kingdom of God" (John 3:5). To understand the signs, one has to be born anew. This "teacher of Israel's" learned gaze at the signs of love does not immediately become love. Nicodemus needs more time to be able to perceive in these signs the wind that "blows where it wills, and you hear the sound of it, but you do not know whence it comes or whither it goes" (John 3:8). The wind of the Spirit blows toward Golgotha and the resurrection, that is, toward man's ultimate and decisive rebirth.

It is significant that immediately after Jesus' dialogue with Nicodemus, St. John recounts one of Christ's most beautiful and profound dialogues with a human being, the conversation with the Samaritan woman at the well. When she glimpses the Truth standing before her, the woman immediately allows it into her moral life. Conversion makes her capable of evangelizing her people.

At the foot of the cross stand the faithful women and the mystic, St. John. The other disciples, frightened by the Master's cruel death and trembling at their own uncertain fate, which they had imagined very differently ("We had hoped that he was the one to redeem Israel" [Luke 24:21]), were not even present at his funeral. They had fled to their hiding places. Jesus was buried, rather, by those who had long kept their ties with him secret for fear of the Jews: Joseph of Arimathea, who was an important member of the Sanhedrin (cf. Mark 15:42-44), and Nicodemus, the Pharisee. Sent by the Risen One, the women find the disciples in hiding and lead them to the empty tomb (cf. Mark 16:7; Luke 24:8-10).

As the Pope said to a woman, the twenty-first century will be the century of woman. We add with André Gide that it will also be the century of mysticism. I repeat: under the cross stand women and the mystic. It is in them that the new evangelization begins anew every day.

Everyone desires evangelization "ever anew," as John Paul II said at the beatification of Bishop Michał Kozal, who was killed in the Dachau concentration camp.[13] Everyone needs a new impetus to stand faithfully by the Truth crucified and risen, to whom every human being belongs.[14] We are afraid of becoming tepid, such that our words and actions become a kind of unsecured check. Evangelization requires a heroic life and an equally heroic thought, since God's "essential work will always remain the Cross and the Resurrection of Christ."[15] Fear and cowardice are always an impediment to God's work. The destiny of Christianity depends on courageous witnesses who know that "man in the full truth of his existence, of his personal being . . . is the primary route that the Church must travel in fulfilling her mission: he is the primary and fundamental way for the Church, the way traced out by Christ himself, the way that leads invariably through the mystery of the Incarnation and the Redemption."[16]

When he leaves his home, the witness to Christ does not abandon his cross. The people who leave their cross in their houses are those who think, as Norwid writes,

> That the beautiful is what pleases
> Because of the egoism of the age and of coteries;
> Until you see that the other person, too,
> And the good itself become egotistical from beauty
> And mortally shrink into what is comfortable
> And the globe quickly becomes too small for man,
> Until a bolt of lightning tears the veil,
> Until a gust of wind is stirred up once again,
> Until the galloping red waves rumble. . . .[17]

Wherever the measure of man and the "center of the universe and history" is not the victory of the Beauty of crucified Truth but rather

---

13. John Paul II, homily at Mass for the end of the National Eucharistic Congress, Warsaw, June 14, 1987.
14. Cf. John Paul II, message to consecrated persons, Częstochowa, June 4, 1997.
15. John Paul II, *Crossing the Threshold of Hope*, p. 134.
16. John Paul II, *Redemptor hominis*, encyclical letter, March 4, 1979, no. 14.
17. Cyprian Norwid, "Promethidion — Bogumił," in *Pisma wszystkie*, vol. 3 (Warsaw: Państwowy Instytut Wydawniczy, 1971), p. 439.

passing success, Love does not fill man's freedom. His personal identity is exhausted in the political calculations of those who administer the State or a political party. From the moment that the Beauty of Truth became human and dwelled among us, then man, too, is a holiness around which world history turns — a holiness safeguarded by those who stand under the cross, immersed in the adoration of Love.

Evangelization as this care for the holiness of man integrates the human person. In the work of evangelization, every omission or, even more, every business dealing with God's word (cf. 2 Cor. 2:17), condemns the human person to the "dissolute living" of the prodigal son in the parable. In a dissolute life, that is, in a life divorced from truth, the "mathematical spirit" *("l'esprit de géométrie")* of which Pascal speaks suffocates the "lively intelligence" of the mind *("l'esprit de finesse")*. Man sees before him not a path to being, but a path to nothingness (Parmenides). "Accustomed to the exact and plain principles of mathematics," he loses himself in matters that require finesse.[18] The "exact and plain principles of mathematics" keep his eyes from recognizing what is before him (cf. Luke 24:16). The new evangelization has to restore a "lively intelligence" to the human mind.

The "specific weight" of the personal act is the love with which the human person responds to and works for Love. *"Pondus meum amor meus; eo feror, quocumque feror"* ["Love is the weight by which I act. To whatever place I go, I am drawn to it by love."].[19] Man converts to the one toward whom he gravitates. With him who is Love, he creates the *communio personarum* and, in it, the *praxis* proper to an adequate anthropology. Those who do not allow themselves to be carried by the weight of love, that is, those who isolate themselves, do an injustice to themselves, to others, and to God. Because they do not journey toward others, they do not journey toward God. They do not change themselves; they do not become other than what they were. They are afraid of difference because it calls them to work for the resurrection — for an ever new evangelization of the world through the cross. Those who, in their fear of difference, avoid the cross and do not change their own life, do not work for the glory of God that man is: *"Gloria Dei homo vivens, homo resurgens!"* "The glory of God is man fully alive, man rising from the dead!"

---

18. Blaise Pascal, *Pensées*, trans. W. F. Trotter, section 1, http://www.ccel.org/ccel/pascal/pensees.i.html.

19. St. Augustine, *Confessions* 13.9.

CHAPTER 4

Marriage and the Family

Every instance of evangelization takes place in dialogue, *dia ton logón*. The word unites person with person. The person's presence to the other person in the word saves them from the misery of solitude. Persons are reborn in one another, giving themselves in the hope never to disappoint one another. The difficulties facing evangelization today have their origin both in the weak faith of Christians, who do not have the courage to entrust themselves to others, and in the secularization of society, which reduces dialogue to an exchange of empty words. Empty words — words in which the person is not present — do not bring people closer to one another. At most, such words convey opinions and hypotheses and confront these with other opinions and hypotheses. In a confrontation of opinions in which some win and others lose, people do not convert to one another. They do not change their lives. Rather, they continue to live as before, focusing on the production of new opinions and hypotheses. The man who is locked into his opinions cannot be reborn; he has no place for this. Held back by their functioning, he does not ask, "Who am I?" but rather, "How do I function?" People interested only in the production and confrontation of opinions and objects (*facere*) are uninterested in their own being, in *esse*. Their life unfolds outside of themselves; nothing happens within them.

Man is reborn when he is present for others in what he says and does, and when others give him their own presence in return. In *Person and Act*, Karol Wojtyła writes of the rebirth of the person in the reciprocal love that is freedom.[1] This rebirth is governed by the logic of the duty that

---

1. Cf. Stanisław Grygiel, "Czyn objawieniem osoby?," *Znak* 23, no. 2-3 = 200-201

John Paul II calls the *"interior discipline of the gift."*[2] The confrontation of opinions is governed by another logic, a mathematical logic too narrow for the human person to be able to live according to its rules.

The "breath of life" (cf. John 2:7) enlivens words and actions in such a way that people are united in them. Each of us receives the truth into his own home when he receives the person in whom this truth reveals itself *(vir qui adest)*. But when we leave the person standing outside and the door locked, the truth cannot come in. How can the door be opened? Even God asks this question, for his Word comes to us and must often knock for a long time at the closed doors of our hearts. The Word of God "came to his own home, and his own people received him not" (John 1:11). We human beings received ourselves in and through this Word, yet we do not cease closing ourselves up before it, making God wait outside. We behave as if we were our own Origin and End.

They who find the "help that corresponds" to them (cf. Gen. 2:20) in a dialogue of love with another person, open their doors to the Word. Together, they keep watch and wait for the Word of the living God, in the hope that it will bring the most fitting "help" to their human love. Alone, this love cannot fully save them from solitude.

It is hard for the Pharisee Nicodemus to understand all this; it is as if he had never before experienced the event that is the union of persons. Fearing the censure of the other Pharisees, he comes to Jesus by night to tell him about the opinions circulating among them about the signs Jesus is performing: "Rabbi, we know that you are a teacher come from God; for no one can do these signs that you do, unless God is with him" (John 3:2). Nicodemus immediately realizes, however, that these opinions about Jesus do not correspond to the Truth that is his Person. The same is true of opinions about every human person. Seeing the signs does not suffice to understand them. We understand them when we set out on the way they point out to us.

Jesus teaches his Person. He neither stops at the signs he has performed nor takes an interest in people's opinions about them. With these signs, he merely reveals his own mission — they reveal who he is for the Father who sent him. Jesus tells Nicodemus this clearly: "Truly, truly, I say to you, unless one is born anew, he cannot see the kingdom of God"

(1971): 200-208. Cf. also Stanisław Grygiel, "Hermeneutyka czynu oraz nowy model świadomości," *Analecta Cracoviensia* 5-6 (1973-74): 139-51.

2. John Paul II, *Letter to Families*, February 2, 1994, no. 14.

(John 3:3). If you do not set out on the Way that is myself, says Christ, you will not see who I am. Trusting completely in his scientific mentality, which moves only with the help of reason, Nicodemus does not rise to the heights where love reigns. He asks Jesus a scientific question: "How can a man be born when he is old? Can he enter a second time into his mother's womb and be born?" (John 3:4). Perceiving how hard it is for this scientist to live and to think poetically, Jesus explains to him in very simple terms that man is reborn — he enters a new life — through a baptism "of water and the Spirit" (John 3:5). New life, the life of the Spirit, begins not so much in the act in which one body unites with another, but in the act whereby persons entrust themselves to one another. This initiation into a new life is the meaning of the baptism of the Spirit.

The scientific mind knows nothing of the spirit of love. This is why the scientific mind does not understand the language of the human body, which is not a language of opinions but a language of spirit and truth. Spirit and truth do not subject themselves to opinions. The human body speaks with the language proper to beauty. Only poets, whose language is song, comprehend it. The spirit, as Jesus tells Nicodemus, moves the human body like a wind, so that this body exists differently than others. You hear the wind, "but you do not know whence it comes or whither it goes; so it is with everyone who is born of the Spirit" (John 3:8). The Spirit and his breath, which moves the human person, dwell in the silence that is alien to the scientific mind.

> You are the Calm, the great Silence,
> free me then from the voice.
> In the tremor of Your being let me shiver
> with the wind,
> borne on the ripe ears of corn.[3]

Nicodemus realizes that Jesus has called his Pharisaic scientific mentality into question, so he asks, "How can this be?" (John 3:9). "Are you a teacher of Israel," Jesus answers in an ironic but friendly tone, "and yet you do not understand this?" (John 3:10). He reveals his own Person to the Pharisee. From now on, the scientist Nicodemus will live in Jesus' presence. Seeing himself in the light of this presence, Nicodemus will per-

---

3. Karol Wojtyła, "Song of the Hidden God: Shores of Silence," in *The Place Within: The Poetry of John Paul II*, trans. Jerzy Peterkiewicz (New York: Random House, 1994), p. 14.

haps mature toward the Word and the Person sent from God. Jesus' acts point to his Person, but it is the Person who interprets the acts and not vice versa. Every person is the hermeneutic principle, the interpretive key, for his own acts. For this reason, only those who unite themselves to the person *dia ton logón* can interpret his acts.

I would dare to say that Christology begins to take form in anthropology, which arrives at the person through his acts and understands the acts in the light of the person. However, it is Christology that explains anthropology and makes it an adequate anthropology. This is the anthropology to which Karol Wojtyła gave rise. He walked toward Jesus through human beings, making them his neighbors, but it was the Person of Jesus who made this anthropological path comprehensible.

We cannot be adequate to the testimony that is Jesus' Person without believing what Jesus says about "earthly things," for how else would we believe in what he says about "heavenly things" (John 3:12)? The miracles Jesus performed reveal the Father's Love. This Love — and only this Love — is what is at issue in Jesus' life and the life of every human being. In *Person and Act*, Karol Wojtyła affirms that the epiphany of every person is the word that is his act and the act that is his word. Only human love and the Love that is God can interpret this articulate deed:

> Love explained all for me,
> all was resolved by love,
> so this love I adore
> wherever it may be.[4]

Jesus places Nicodemus before the Love that is God: "For God so loved the world that he gave his only Son, that whoever believes in him should not perish but have eternal life" (John 3:16). Jesus places Nicodemus before the necessity of seeing that God loves man so much that, incomprehensibly, he "had" to become incarnate so that when man sees the God-man, he might also know and understand himself. So that man, too, might become love. Jesus reveals to man the greatness of human dignity — the dignity for which God himself "had" to die.

After this nocturnal encounter with Jesus, the scientifically minded Pharisee appears in the Gospel only once, as Jesus' body is taken down from the cross. He brought myrrh and aloes, the Gospel tells us, to pre-

---

4. Wojtyła, "Song of the Hidden God: Shores of Silence," p. 6.

pare the body for burial. Did the cross become for him a door through which he entered the country of Love? Did he mature enough to cross the threshold not to a new opinion, but to a new life? Did he change his way of thinking *(metanoia)*? Did he unite knowledge and love? The Evangelist, who knew Nicodemus, does not tell us. People caught in their own science find it difficult to look on temporal things in the light of the eternal. It is difficult for those who listen to the voices of the earth and their own time to hear in them the voice of eternity. How and where can one learn to hear the voice of the Eternal in time?

Norwid tells us that once, as he was traveling by mule toward Grottaferrata,[5] he met a peasant on a path near Castel Gandolfo and stopped to speak with him. When the bells rang for the Angelus, "both of us took off our hats. This shared, brief prayer introduced us into dialogue."[6]

The world becomes comprehensible for those who, when they ask the question about man, ask the question about God and vice versa — in asking the question about God, they ask the question about man. The philosophy of the question, "Who is man?" and the prayer of the question, "Who is God for man?," are the fundamental principles for understanding everything that is and that has meaning insofar as it is a sign of something greater. This is why the God-man is the center of the universe and of history (cf. *Redemptor hominis*, 1).

In the void between people, one can discern neither God nor man. In Wojtyła's play, *The Jeweler's Shop*, Anna sees the face of her husband Stefan in the Bridegroom who unexpectedly passes by just as she is struggling with herself and with her marital faith. The jeweler, to whom she had tried to sell her wedding ring, told her, "This ring does not weigh anything . . . and I cannot make it show even a milligram. Your husband must be alive — in which case neither of your rings, taken separately, will weigh anything" on the scales that "weigh . . . man's entire being and fate."[7] The weight of the rings is "the proper weight of man," which is "heavier . . . and more intangible" than any other weight.[8] Anna laments,

---

5. A small town in the province of Rome with a monastery that is a place of pilgrimage.

6. Cyprian Norwid, "Białe kwiaty," *Pisma wszystkie*, vol. 6 (Warsaw: Państwowy Instytut Wydawniczy, 1971), p. 193.

7. Karol Wojtyła, *The Jeweler's Shop*, trans. Boleslaw Taborski (San Francisco: Ignatius, 1992), p. 52.

8. Wojtyła, *The Jeweler's Shop*, p. 37.

> When I then ran, so full of hidden hope,
> toward the Bridegroom so suddenly promised,
> I saw Stefan's face.
> Must he have that face for me?
> Why? Why?[9]

Love opens us to the coming of the Bridegroom, who bears the face of the person with whom we are united in a common destiny. Love for another person always aims higher, at the Bridegroom; it awaits him. In the "we" of interpersonal love, the "we" is accomplished in which man becomes ever more like the God-man. Humanity is humanity to the extent that it is more than humanity. Love that aims this far, not the *mens*, or scientific mind, reveals who man is. The principle of the hermeneutic of the question about man has to be greater than science and its hypothetical opinions. For love does not live from opinions.

Love is awakened in the encounter, when we human beings are invested with the rays of the beautiful that emanate from the other person. The trembling we experience in that moment is the beginning of eternity. Overcome by the presence of eternity in time, we begin to speak with the marvelous, even supernatural language of love — a language with which we tell of the life that is death and the death through which we enter into new life. We tell of "that amazement which will become the essence/of eternity."[10] We articulate this with our uncalculated presence to others and our silence, which is the word most adequate to eternity. Silence touches both the Transcendence of God and the transcendence of man.

By itself, thought will not cross the threshold at which Nicodemus hesitates. And yet the latter is not like the Pharisee who proclaims his good actions before the altar. He is more like the publican who, "standing far off, would not even lift up his eyes to heaven, but beat his breast, saying, 'God, be merciful to me, a sinner'" (Luke 18:13). To people whose heads are bowed, "Jesus, the Good Shepherd, continues to say . . . *Do not be afraid. I am with you.* 'I am with you always, to the close of the age' (Mt 28:20). What is the source of this strength? What is the reason for our certainty that you are with us, even though they put you to death, O Son of God, and you died like any other human being? . . . The Evangelist says:

---

9. Wojtyła, *The Jeweler's Shop*, p. 68.
10. Wojtyła, "Song of the Hidden God: Shores of Silence," p. 4.

'He loved them to the end' (Jn 13:1). Thus do you love us, you who are the First and the Last, the Living One; you who died and are alive for evermore (cf. Rev 1:17-18)."[11]

Jesus helps Nicodemus, but he does so in such a way that the Pharisee's frightened heart has time to mature to a courage not of words but of blood. "If the word did not convert you, the blood will," says the martyr St. Stanislas in Wojtyła's poem, "Stanislas."[12] Death opens the eyes of all who gaze on it and on whom it gazes. It takes courage to come to the foot of the cross and, with the help of faith, to manage to see new life in the dead man and to anoint him with myrrh and aloes for this life. Such courage is given only to the man who is amazed by the gift of love. How great must have been Nicodemus' amazement at the person of Jesus!

Jesus speaks in a different way with each human being, for every human being is unrepeatable. But it is always the same Spirit of God who descends on every unrepeatable man, to convince him that the "Tree" that remains while the world changes must be wounded. Man can be grafted onto the tree only through the wound.[13] *"Stat crux dum volvitur mundus"* [The cross stands while the world turns].

Gazing at Jesus, we are moved, but Jesus is also moved, gazing at us. He is moved like the Samaritan traveler who saw an unfortunate stranger wounded and lying by the side of the road (cf. Luke 10:33). The Samaritan did not ask the man in need to what social class he belonged. He did not ask others for their opinions about him. He was moved with pity and, unlike the priest and the Levite, entered into a person-to-person dialogue with him. The Samaritan's compassion freed him from opinions *(doxa)* and opened for him the way to knowledge *(episteme)* of the truth in man. The unfortunate stranger helped the Samaritan to discover that he, too, belonged to the true and the good. This belonging knows no relativism.

People who are moved by one another come out of their own immanence. Journeying toward the transcendent reality that reveals itself in them, they journey toward the Transcendence their "restless hearts" desire. Dwelling in one another as one dwells in one's family home, where love and freedom rule, they prepare themselves to dwell in the Father's house. People who are moved by one another have the Future before

---

11. John Paul II, *Letter to Families*, 18.
12. Karol Wojtyła, "Stanislas," in *Place Within*, p. 181.
13. Karol Wojtyła, "Easter Vigil, 1966: II: A Tale of a Wounded Tree," in *Place Within*, pp. 126-28.

them. This Future continually surprises them, reawakening in them an astonished admiration for the life that conquers death.

Those who are not united by their wonder at the beauty of the person form a mass of individuals, entangled in an artificial world of calculations and hounded by bankers and politicians. They bear a yoke made up of predicates, with which they present themselves — as if these predicates were their own identity. Such people are formed in what Pascal calls the "mathematical spirit," in which two-dimensional figures communicate with one another via predicated qualities that are increasingly mathematically formal. They do not know how to govern themselves. Forming friendships and marriages with these qualities rather than with the person, they create ties *ad experimentum*, in which the hypothetical *ratum* occupies the place that ought to be occupied by an unconditional *consummatum est*.

Philosophy, which today is based on predication as the foundation of thought and of life, deforms the human person and his world. It does not recognize differences between people beyond those with which this philosophy itself determines their social and individual *praxis*. Predicated differences do not unite persons. Predicates cannot discover true unity between persons, but only construct a temporary unity *ad experimentum*. So we should not be surprised if they do not oblige anyone to fidelity until death, but rather make this fidelity dependent on circumstances. It is also natural that this kind of predication eliminates the word "betrayal" from our vocabulary. One does not betray predicates, one simply changes them.

According to such logic, the person does not betray another person in friendship, marriage, or the nation, but simply substitutes a new predicate for an old one if in the old he no longer finds a "help" that corresponds to him (cf. Gen. 2:18-20). (Post)modernity calls progress not the deepening of the mutual fidelity of persons, but the continual invention of new predicates, which we impose on animals and things. Postmodern man is an Adam who reduces animals and people to the names he invents.

Adam's metaphysical and anthropological error — the Prometheanism that allows him to treat everyone and everything *ad libitum* — cancels out sexual difference, which unites persons in "one flesh" (cf. Gen. 2:24). This error destroys the foundation on which homes are built — the "homes" that are marriage and the family, as well as society. Those who do not see unity in difference construct artificial homes for people. The unity of persons cannot be constructed. Any such construction will always be a hypothesis *ad experimentum*. This is always what happens to friendships, marriages, and families that have been reduced to hypotheses to be verified.

How do we free ourselves from the misery of relativism, which is encouraged by the Pharaonic abundance of predicates? "The rib which the LORD God had taken from the man he made into a woman and brought her to the man," who, upon seeing her, uttered this cry full of wonder: "This at last is bone of my bones and flesh of my flesh!" (Gen. 2:22-23). Human freedom arises in the person's continual wonderment at the beauty of the other person, who differs from himself so much that she reveals to him the incarnate truth of his earthly being.

Wonder forms an essential moment for the adequate anthropology proposed by Karol Wojtyła. In man's wonderment at the beauty of woman and woman's wonderment at the beauty of man, the moral experience of the human person takes place. This experience creates the space for knowledge of the truth through love. Wonder signifies the defeat of postmodernity in Adam.

At times this focus on predication is even understood to be the foundation of ontology, deforming (masculine) man with a hypothetical feminine predicate and woman with a hypothetical masculine predicate. When man and woman are deformed, then marriage, the family, the nation, and even the Church follow suit, insofar as the human enters into the latter's constitution. This Promethean, anti-divine, and authoritarian way of thinking about the human being eliminates the differences between persons. This in turn allows the person to be treated *ad libitum*.

* * *

"We must wonder! We must create an environment of wonder! We must create a climate of wonder! This task is closest to the family. . . . Wonder is needed so that beauty might enter into human life, into society and the nation. This beauty is the foundation and the creative moment of the culture. It is impossible to create culture by administrative means. These means can only destroy it. . . . We need to marvel at everything that is found in man."[14] Karol Wojtyła's adequate anthropology is born of man's

---

14. Karol Wojtyła, homily at the inauguration of the tenth Festival of Choral and Religious Music "Sacrosong 78," Jasna Góra, September 17, 1978. I cite from Karol Wojtyła, *Muzyka: Antologia tekstów* (Krakow: Akademia Muzyczna, 2011), p. 77.

wonder at the covenant between the promise that is the breath of the human person's beauty, and the hope that enlivens him who marvels at this beauty, allowing it to pervade him. "Love is enthusiasm rather than pensiveness."[15] Those who do not marvel at beauty do not rise above their hypotheses or above the earth. They do not live in hope, since only the beauty of the person promises us eternity — an eternity that their eyes, closed by predicates, are unable to see.

Beauty leads people out of the cave of opinions and hypotheses on the path that Diotima explains to Socrates in Plato's *Symposium*. This path leads the human person to the eternal Beauty through his wonderment first at the beautiful body of another person, then at his beautiful thoughts and actions.

The task of the new evangelization consists in teaching people to see themselves in the light of personal differences — especially in the light of that fundamental difference, sexual difference. In the space it creates, the beauty of love is revealed. This beauty allows us to glimpse the truth in which we can dwell forever. A deformed beauty profanes the truth of man. (Post)modernity imposes tolerance of this profanation, whereas it forbids tolerating those who ask for and seek the truth and freedom.

In the space of sexual difference, man and woman give themselves to one another according to the logic of the beauty of the flesh, of thought and of actions, that is, according to the "interior discipline of the gift." The beauty of the logic of the gift, which is revealed in sexual difference, orients the body, thoughts, and action of man and woman to the Beauty reflected in them. In the wonder provoked in their persons by the beauty of their bodies, thoughts, and actions, the path is opened to marriage. Here man and woman initiate one another into a new life, open to receiving other persons.

The gift does not come according to the law of necessity. If it did, it would not be a gift but rather the product of *facere* — of their making. Both the rebirth of the person and the coming of a human being into the world are mysteries of love, not problems of justice. Not all marriages receive this, but all marriages must be ready to receive it. Love is a greater and therefore more difficult justice, known only by those who entrust themselves to it. A lack of love, which in no way claims to receive the gift and makes no demands, cancels out all realism in our vision of man. It thus cancels out the very foundation of justice. It keeps the person from

---

15. Wojtyła, *Jeweler's Shop*, p. 38.

Marriage and the Family

setting out on the paschal path to rebirth in the other person. Many scientists do not understand this. In the name of a justice separated from love, they invent "idiotic" marriages and families, in the Greek sense of this word. Love and birth calculated by reason profane the dignity of man.

John Paul II spoke of marital love as an event that participates in the act of the creation of man. It also participates in the entrustment of the world to him. Working in the world, the human person grows in love — that is, he becomes ever more love. Love and work form such a unity that when this unity is destroyed, love becomes a game and work becomes exhausting labor. Consequently, the value of both love and work is measured by the utility of the moment (utilitarianism), pleasure (hedonism), and knowing how to construct ever new hypotheses (learned erudition). A "legion" (cf. Luke 8:30) of ethics that serve the separation of love from work rely on decrees that change with passing fashions or bow to political correctness.

Love, especially marital and familial love, does not consist in subjecting oneself to circumstances and their demands. Rather, it consists in the struggle of the gift with the gift that is beyond decrees. The greater the love in marriage and the family, the less people need to be reminded of the commandments engraved in human nature in defense of this love. In love, people's lives unfold beyond ethically distinct good and evil. It is not ethics that governs life in God the Father and God the Son, but rather Love. The love in marriage and the family is an image of that Love.

In the dialogue of marriage, which is created "in the image and likeness" of the divine dialogue of Father and Son, woman enters into the sanctuary of man and man into the sanctuary of woman such that they become "one flesh" (cf. Gen. 2:24). The destruction of the unity of their bodies prolongs the tragedy of Adam and Eve's primordial fall. We human beings cannot reconstruct the gift of unity that has been destroyed. We must wait for a new breath of the Spirit in truth. He moves us to receive a new gift, this time for a still greater love and unity. The same can be said for the damaged unity of the Church. I would say even more: the question of how to help those who have destroyed the gift of their marital unity is at bottom the ecumenical question of unity for the divided Church.

In those who have destroyed the unity they received, the truth does not reveal itself, for truth has the character of communion. It is revealed and actualized where people are present to one another (*"vir qui adest"*). With a smile, a tear, a caress, or words, persons reveal to one another that they are knowable *(verum)* and loveable *(bonum)*. In a unity that has been destroyed, the epiphany of the true and the good is deformed. "Man and woman, made in the divine image, were meant from the beginning to prolong in time the dialogue of love that exists in the heart of God. They were meant to transmit his creative word, which is a font of life, in the same way that the flame of a torch passes on the fire with which it was lit" (cf. *Summa Contra Gentiles* 2, 46).[16]

The human person comes into the world from "Nothingness." That is, he comes from the Love inaccessible to human eyes, which is God. God's Love creates the human person with his divine Word, which is present in the dialogue of love that unites father and mother. In their dialogue, the fire flames forth of the Spirit of the truth of man who must become God. Love is not a juxtaposition of two flames. It is their unity, *"una caro."* The flame of a torch, reborn from the flame of another, illuminates its surroundings. A miserable darkness would fall over the world if man did not say to woman and woman to man, "I am you and you are me!" In societies where "subject-subject" relations dominate between human beings, there is light, but darkness prevails wherever people's lives are subjected to the dialectical relation of subject and object.

Marriages built on the dualism of subject and object produce Sartre's hell: "Hell is other people" *(L'enfer, c'est les autres!)*. Because they do not know how to die to themselves, people who are not united by ties of love do not mature to the resurrection. They do not know how to be a task, a *munus*, for one another. Since they do not live *cummunere*, with the task that is the other person, they do not create *communio personarum*, the communion of persons. They are not *muniti*, defended *(munio, -ire*, to defend). Deprived of a personal task, life becomes a desperate sadness. "No one is as sad as I. . . . Now I gaze in myself and see that I am . . . dead. Did I say I was sad? I lied. The desert is neither gay nor sad, that incalculable nothingness of sand under the clear nothingness of heaven: it is sinister. Ah! I would give my kingdom to shed a tear!"[17] Aegistheus, who speaks these words in Sartre's play, dominates social and political mechanisms and therefore human beings; he seeks to make his presence to others, and theirs to him, superfluous. His life unravels into miserable thought and miserable time. It is true that Wojtyła said that man lives the experience

---

16. John Paul II, homily at the concelebration for Christian families in the Stadium of Cali, Cali, Colombia, July 4, 1986.

17. Jean-Paul Sartre, *The Flies*, act 2, scene 2.

of the other person from the outside, but he lives it in the knowledge that is love *(agere)*. Other people open Wojtyła to heaven. He could say, *"Le ciel, c'est les autres!"* — heaven is other people! Heaven "happens" in the encounter (in Greek, *symballein*) of person with person; the encounter has a symbolical nature. Since hell distances person from person *(diaballein)*, hell has a diabolical nature. For this reason, hell is the total negation of poetry.

If we want the new evangelization to help the Church to be reborn, it must have a care for the love that unites man with woman. Karol Wojtyła learned to love human love from laypeople. Participating in their full, reciprocal self-entrustment in the life of marriage and the family allowed him to enter more profoundly into the mystery of love and freedom. Laypeople taught him to see that in spousal love, heaven appears in this world — or else hell, where this love is lacking. Love, even our defective love, represents the model of the Church, just as the Church is constituted by the Love of God and the love that we desire to be, despite the flaws that contaminate our desire.

In this way — and only in this way — the new evangelization will care also for the State. The State is an expression of marriages and families. It collapses when they collapse, or when they are denatured. "The family belongs to the most original and sacred patrimonies of humanity! It comes before the State, which is bound to recognize it and, on the basis of easily comprehensible ethical and social evidence, has the duty to protect it and never to obscure it. Whatever threatens the family, threatens man."[18] A State that threatens the family, threatens man.

John Paul II's vision of marriage and the family was founded on the one hand on the revelation that is God's Incarnate Word present in the Church, and on the other hand on the truth of man that is revealed in the person's moral experience. Aristotle comes close to this when he writes, "Man is by nature a pairing creature even more than he is a political creature, inasmuch as the family is an earlier and more fundamental institution than the State."[19] For both Aristotle and John Paul II, marriage and the family are at the basis of society and not society at the basis of the family. In the *Eudemian Ethics*, Aristotle writes, "In the family are found the origins and the source of friendship, so-

---

18. John Paul II, *Regina Coeli*, April 17, 1994.
19. Aristotle, *Nicomachean Ethics* 1162a, trans. H. Rackham, Loeb Classical Library (Cambridge, MA: Harvard University Press, 2003), p. 503.

ciety and justice."[20] For both Aristotle and John Paul II, the good of marriage and the family are the State's raison d'être and not vice versa. The person, marriage, and the family precede the State. They are *prius tempore et natura*. So the State cannot treat them as objects of its own operations with impunity. It must serve them. The politicization of marriage and the family — and thus the definition of these realities by the State — destroys the latter's very foundation. The State cannot exist without marriage and the family, whereas marriage and the family can exist in their fullness without the State.

The quality of marriages and families, as well as their generous love, decides the quality of the State. "When the value of the family is threatened because of social and economic pressures, we will stand up and reaffirm that the family is 'necessary not only for the private good of every person, but also for the common good of every society, nation and state,'" John Paul II said forcefully in a homily delivered on the National Mall in Washington, D.C., on October 7, 1979. I don't think I am distancing myself from his thought if I affirm that marriage and the family are the world's first citizens. They radiate into the world the beauty that the world cannot understand.

Crises of the State usually result from crises of persons, marriages, families, and nations. For the good of the State, citizens have the duty and therefore also the right to say "No!" to laws that do not acknowledge the priority of the person, marriage, the family, and the nation over politics. The roots of what has real priority reach into eternity. Precisely for this reason, it is not permitted for the person, marriage, the family, and the nation to kneel before the State, since they owe their identity not to the State but to God. To kneel before the State means to live in the stupidity proper to idolatry (cf. Deut. 32:19). "They have stirred me to jealousy with what is no god; they have provoked me with their idols. So I will stir them to jealousy with those who are no people; I will provoke them with a foolish nation" (Deut. 32:21). Battling with one another, the gods of the State provoke conflict not only between States but also between nations, families, and marriages. These idols silence the laws that give life and unity to society. Every tiny god seeks to prevail against its like. I recall here the words spoken by John Paul II at the end of an encounter in 1994 with the faithful of the parish of Santa Maria Madre dell'Ospitalità in Rome. He told them that he was returning to Rome "to fight a program, a project

---

20. Aristotle, *Eudemian Ethics* 1242b.

of the United Nations, which wants to destroy the family. My God! The United Nations! I say simply, reconsider! Convert! If you are the United Nations, you cannot divide and destroy!"[21]

States that deprive persons, marriages, families, and nations of sovereignty weaken themselves morally and thus also politically and economically. Seeking sovereignty for themselves in effective calculations, they subject themselves to *technē*, to a technique and a technology that function as if they were the first and last subject of society and its members. No one can dominate technique who is not governed by the "great question" *(magna questio)* of the meaning of human life. No one can foresee the consequences of a technological libertinism. When politics and economics are not founded on the question of the meaning of human life but rather on the development of technical science, they build a world hostile to man. As John Paul II told us, the only thing that can save us from such a world is the civilization of love. Heidegger was perfectly aware of the dangers inherent in technology. In an interview published posthumously in the German magazine *Der Spiegel*, the philosopher said that in a state of affairs created by technology, only gods can save us. I would add that only a new, great, and very dramatic exodus from this state of affairs can save us.

The experience of the cruel trampling of the dignity of persons, marriages, and families on the part of Nazism and communism made it clear to Wojtyła that in marriage and the family, a decisive battle was being fought for truth and for freedom — a battle for the dignity of the human person. In marriage and the family, people rediscover their humanity. We should not be surprised, then, if all tyrants try to destroy marriages and families in order to impose their own will on society unhindered.

Freedom and sovereignty are difficult gifts, which societies that have interiorly collapsed do not know how to handle. Societies administered by functionaries of the "master-slave" dialectic do not know that love and freedom are duties of the person. In the "slaves" who rebel against the "masters," duties become claims, which they call "individual rights."

The duty of love and freedom and the right to these orient the human person to the God from whom they come. Only God is Love and Freedom. The vision of the land promised and entrusted to human love and freedom ought to orient our exodus from slavery and solitude. The land

---

21. John Paul II, address during pastoral visit to the parish of Santa Maria Madre dell'Ospitalità, Rome, April 17, 1994.

Discovering the Human Person

promised and entrusted to us shows itself in those marriages and families in which the statement "I am" has only one predicate: "I am because I am loved." This is, so to speak, an existential predicate. The maturity of the human person consists in the fact that he sees himself as sent to others. The mature man knows that he is mission (the Latin word *missus* means "sent").

In his pastoral work, John Paul II shared the lives of marriages and families with great gentleness. He respected their freedom and sovereignty. Together with them, he sought to know the mission that God had given as much to them as to him who accompanied them. He proposed the Holy Family of Nazareth, *"the beginning of countless other holy families,"*[22] as the model of every family. He bowed his head before the holiness of these families; this was the attitude with which he spoke with them about the essential problems of their lives. In their difficult moments, he spoke more with his silent presence than with words. Like Bishop Jan Pietraszko, he asked them to help him. In giving this help, they discovered that their difficulties resolved themselves. Both Wojtyła and Pietraszko behaved as Jesus did with the Samaritan woman at Jacob's well. Before helping her to resolve the problem of her tangled loves, he asked her to help him: "Give me a drink" (John 4:7).

Jesus' question causes the woman to marvel: "How is it that you, a Jew, ask a drink of me, a woman of Samaria?" (John 4:9). Jesus had done something surprising. He behaved as if he were not a Jew, "for Jews have no dealings with Samaritans." Wonder at his person opens the door of the woman's interiority to Jesus. Still, he does not enter immediately. He waits for an invitation: "If you knew the gift of God, and who it is that is saying to you, 'Give me a drink,' you would have asked him, and he would have given you living water" (John 4:10). In order to understand what Jesus is saying to her, the woman gives a twofold reply. She says that he has nothing with which to draw water and yet wants to give her water from a deep well. And she does not know but wishes to know whether he who is speaking is greater than their father Jacob, from whom the Samaritans received the gift of the well. The woman has clearly understood one thing: that he who just asked her to help him and now wants to help her is not just an ordinary man. He speaks to her with a language that points to something that cannot be found in the content of the words. The woman senses that Jesus' words about the water he can give mean what they say,

---

22. John Paul II, *Letter to Families*, no. 23.

and yet they mean much more. These words raise her to an unknown reality, which she desires as she desires water from the well.

In her dialogue with Jesus, the Samaritan woman is resplendent with the mystery of Woman, who, knowing the pains of childbirth, glimpses in the mystery of pain the mystery of man's spiritual rebirth.[23] Scientific-mindedness does not keep her eyes from seeing. Thus Jesus tells her and not Nicodemus about the "living water" he gives to those who ask him. The Samaritan woman does not hesitate for an instant: "Sir, give me this water, that I may not thirst, nor come here to draw" (John 4:15). With her obedient *fiat mihi* to the "gift of God," she shows us the way to man's renewed birth.

Every human being requires a change of life, that is, a conversion to the truth that begins to unveil itself in the gift. Confronted with Jesus' request that she go call her husband and come back with him, the Samaritan woman understands the condition for being able to receive the "gift of God." Jesus does not criticize her. His presence in this dialogue with the woman is only a light, thanks to which she sees herself in truth. She confesses precisely this truth about herself, without going into particulars: "I have no husband" (John 4:17). It is Jesus who tells her the details, for he knew from the beginning what was happening in the woman's interior. Astonished but at the same time liberated by truth's work upon her erring love, the woman asks Jesus where one is to adore God, on this mountain or in Jerusalem. She knows now that a love that does not orient a person to God is not love but a substitute for it. She understands the greatness of Jesus' words when he says that God must be adored "in spirit and truth." But since she is unable to interpret them, she can only confess her own faith to Jesus: "I know that Messiah is coming (he who is called Christ); when he comes, he will show us all things" (John 4:25). To this woman's faith, hope, and desire for love, Jesus clearly reveals the truth of his being on earth: "I who speak to you am he" (John 4:26).

The woman goes without hesitation to her people with her *Magnificat*. She becomes an apostle. Many of them convert to Jesus.

Woman is sent to society so that with her presence, she might defend humanity against degeneration into a mass of solitary individuals, whom

---

23. Karol Wojtyła, *Radiation of Fatherhood*, in *The Collected Plays and Writings on Theater*, trans. Boleslaw Taborski (Berkeley: University of California Press, 1987), pp. 361-62.

no one defends against the "viper."[24] In the mass of individuals, there are neither parents nor children who say to one another, "You are mine!," that is, "I belong to you!" Thanks to the woman who knows how to receive the gift, society becomes a family of persons who are present to one another and who defend one another from the "viper." John Paul II knew that woman is owed a love full of gratitude.

I will never forget what I witnessed during the 1991 Synod of European Bishops at the Vatican. During a plenary session of all the Cardinals and bishops, in the presence of John Paul II, five laypeople gave interventions. They were four men and one woman, Irina Alberti Iłowajskaja, a well-known Russian intellectual. After we spoke, each of us approached the Holy Father, who was seated, to greet him. When it was Ms. Iłowajskaja's turn to greet the Pope, he stood up, to general astonishment. A little later he told me, "I can't remain seated when I'm speaking with a woman."

The woman's maternal love illumines for her children the path that leads to the father.[25] Woman, the mother, shows the way *(hodighitrìa)*. Woman, the mother, shows her child to perceive a Great Meaning in himself, that is, the Father.[26] "We follow the traces of the Meaning."[27] They who seek this Meaning adore God in Spirit and truth. Children who live ignorant of their father forget that they are brothers. They do not know how to be children.[28]

A calling into question of the woman and mother is and always will be a crisis of society. It is her voice that helps us to seek the Source of "living water" for the family and society. "Source, where are you?!" John Paul II calls in his *Roman Triptych*.[29] Isn't he perhaps joining the Samaritan woman in invoking the "living water"?

With the help of woman, the human person seeks the Origin that is the Father. Woman knows the human person's beginning, which points to the way that leads to the end. When she speaks of the beginning and end, she does so together with the mother of the seven brothers in the second book of Maccabees, in such a way that the beginning and the end

---

24. Cf. Wojtyła, *Radiation of Fatherhood*, p. 348.
25. Cf. Wojtyła, *Radiation of Fatherhood*, p. 362.
26. Cf. Wojtyła, *Radiation of Fatherhood*, p. 347.
27. Wojtyła, *Radiation of Fatherhood*, p. 349.
28. Wojtyła, *Radiation of Fatherhood*, p. 339.
29. John Paul II, *The Poetry of John Paul II: Roman Triptych*, trans. Jerzy Peterkiewicz (Washington, DC: USCCB, 2003), p. 9.

point to the mystery of the human person's Origin and End. Hölderlin writes,

> A mystery are those of pure origin.
> Even song may hardly unveil it.
> For as you began, so you will remain.[30]

A ray of the mystery of the Origin illumines the person who is the infant in its mother's womb. It first illumines the understanding of the woman-mother. She then transmits this illumination to the father so that through his own fatherhood, he will walk together with the child toward their one, shared Father. The human person will never move from "this child's place,"[31] for he is the history of the Father whose "beginning is lost in the darkness"[32] and who develops in the child through the mother, so that the child (cf. Monica in *Radiation of Fatherhood*) is the unity of father and mother.[33] With the help of the mother's *fiat mihi*, the child sets out into the will of the father who generates. Entering into this will, the child is born from the father, because she understands that she has been chosen by him.[34] She is born with the help of the mother's *fiat*. Through the mother, fatherhood radiates into the child. When man and woman

> ... become "one flesh"
> — that wondrous union —
> on the horizon there appears the mystery of
>   fatherhood and motherhood.
> — They return to the source of life within them.
> — They return to the Beginning.
> — Adam knew his wife
> and she conceived and gave birth.
> They know that they have crossed the threshold
> of the greatest responsibility![35]

---

30. Friedrich Hölderlin, "The Rhine," *Poems and Fragments*, trans. Michael Hamburger, 4th ed. (London: Anvil Press Poetry, 2004), p. 501.
   31. Wojtyła, *Radiation of Fatherhood*, p. 351.
   32. Wojtyła, *Radiation of Fatherhood*, p. 344.
   33. Wojtyła, *Radiation of Fatherhood*, p. 345.
   34. Wojtyła, *Radiation of Fatherhood*, p. 354.
   35. John Paul II, *Roman Triptych*, p. 21.

Once they have crossed this threshold, they understand that "[l]ove is not an adventure. It has the taste of the whole man. It has his weight. And the weight of his whole fate. It cannot be a single moment."[36] Bearing this weight, they glimpse the primordial, beautiful "nakedness" of their own being in the Origin. They recover an awareness of what they are and thus also of what they ought to become. At their end, the ray of Love that once fell upon their conception by their father in their mother's womb does not separate them or condemn them to solitude. It is not by chance that immediately after being elected Pope, the author of *Love and Responsibility* united the Church's teaching about the Origin (the act of creation) with its teaching about the beauty of the love that unites man and woman. In conversations with John Paul II, the theme almost always surfaced of a responsible love, the beauty of which allows human work to rediscover its proper meaning. For him, the love on which marriages and families are built is also that on which is built "the Church: the lowest depth of my existence/and its peak,/ . . . — the root which I thrust/into the past and the future alike."[37] This love is our homeland. "When I think my Country — /I express what I am, anchoring my roots."[38] Without this homeland, every marriage, family, and society will be nothing but a juxtaposition of calculated and calculating individuals.

Marriage, the family, and the nation are spiritual events. In other words, they are events in the freedom of faith, the freedom of hope, and the freedom of love. Spiritual events cannot be reduced to institutional structures, even if the former need to take on the latter's form. Spiritual events transcend administration. For this reason, they confer on institutional structures life and strength, but only when the structures have a care for such events. State constitutions that are not rooted in the spiritual events of faith, hope, and love make arbitrary decisions regarding the functioning of these institutions and impose a direction on the lives of the citizens. Plato probably feared precisely this when he wrote that the State must be governed by wise and just men. That is, it must be governed by *philosophers* (lovers of wisdom), because only they know what laws are: rights that are derived from duties *(munera)*. Only they understand the nature of decrees, the Origin and End of which is the fickle will of the powerful.

---

36. Wojtyła, *Jeweler's Shop*, p. 60.
37. Wojtyła, "Stanislas," p. 179.
38. Wojtyła, "Thinking My Country," in *Place Within*, p. 141.

Marriage and the Family

Knowing from pastoral experience that marriage and the family mature toward their truth through the entire lifetime of a husband and wife, Fr. Wojtyła stressed that the couple needs the patience and courage we must beg from God (cf. Rom. 15:5). He himself, a sign of God's presence in their lives as a priest, remained faithful in his nearness to them even after Christ called him to the see of Peter. He did not abandon those who had taught him to love human love. He continued to learn how to love this love to the end of his life. This perseverance of pastors with the marriages and families they accompany is what married couples, parents, and children ask for. If marital and parental love does not provoke admiration in pastors, people will not find in the new evangelization a "help" that corresponds to them (Gen. 2:18).

Marital love is born in the beauty of sexual difference. Along this line of demarcation, which simultaneously distinguishes and unites man and woman, love creates in them a shared flesh, moral conscience, and responsibility. Together, man and woman see how infinitely each of them transcends themselves. They understand the meaning of their desire for the infinite, which unites them. "For many years I have lived like a man exiled from my deeper personality yet condemned to probe it."[39] Descending together into their depths, husband and wife each mature in their "we" to the "I" of their own person. They enter into the "abyss" beyond speech[40] — beyond the language of the body, thoughts, and actions — where a mysterious abyss opens of the love that "moves the sun and the other stars."[41] Along the demarcating line of sexual difference, *"the genealogy of the person is inscribed in the very biology of generation."*[42] So we should not marvel that the choice of a companion on the path that leads to this divine abyss is a sacred choice that binds us forever. Man pays with his whole self for the abyss of truth and freedom. They demand of him heroism of thought and of life.

By orienting woman to man and man to woman, sexual difference introduces them into dialogue. In other words, it introduces them to the spiritual life. It "counsels" them to establish a covenant in which each of them is simultaneously a promise for the other and a hope placed in him. All other agreements, including political and economic agreements, are

---

39. Wojtyła, *Radiation of Fatherhood*, p. 335.

40. Wojtyła, "Thinking My Country: I Reach the Heart of the Drama," in *Place Within*, p. 145.

41. Dante Alighieri, *The Divine Comedy: Paradise*, canto 33, line 145.

42. John Paul II, *Letter to Families*, no. 9.

or ought to be made in "the image and likeness" of this covenant. Mystics and poets describe even the covenant that binds God and man with language born from the experience of sexual difference and from the dialogue of promise and call with hope and response. When we call sexual difference into question, we condemn ourselves to treating marriage, the family, the nation, and the Church — and therefore also ourselves — in the same way as technological libertinism.

The generous union of man and woman in sexual difference forms a paradigm for the generous knowledge that takes place in the union of the knower and the known. In such knowledge, both the knower and the known are reborn "in spirit and truth," that is, in the adoration of God. Thus knowledge of the truth and of freedom has divine-human dimensions in the human person. They point him to the nuptial faiths that, separated, have no weight. No one — no organization and no State — can change the divine-human dimensions of the human person, imposing on him their own conception of truth and freedom. The sovereignty of the human person derives from his belonging to another person and ultimately, to the Person of God, not from his belonging to this or that institution. That which is divine in the human person confers on him this freedom and this sovereignty.

The atheism that results from this anthropological error rejects the human person's belonging to God. This allows the functionaries of this or that power to define truth, freedom, and love, changing the content of these words according to circumstances. They treat people's bodies according to the same circumstances, imposing thoughts on them and orienting their actions. In Europe, it seems that the Spartans were the first to change the contents of words in conquered Athens. Once chaos had been introduced into the minds of the Athenian citizens, the conquerors could manipulate them more easily. The Nazis and communists did something similar. They knew that torture and assassinations alone were not enough to dominate the human person. One also had to dominate language, manipulating it in such a way that it no longer refers to what really is but to what they wanted people to believe. People lost in the language in which they dwell also lose their orientation in personal, social, and political life. They do not understand themselves and are unable to communicate with others. They lose their trust in one another. Fear dominates their language and their behavior, to the point that they cease to think.

The new evangelization ought to restore words to the reality to which they belong. Today, almost no one but the Church wants to see what the functionaries of power are able to do with words such as love, fidelity, freedom, marriage, family, and nation. The Church remembers that the content of these great words does not come from reasoning or calculation. It arises in the person who is astonished at the beauty of love for what really is, and so sings the Love that is God. If the Church stopped remembering this, we would end up constructing a new tower of Babel that would collapse over us. The Church must teach people to speak in a way that is adequate to reality.

The choice of woman on the part of man and of man on the part of woman concretizes the mission with which each of them is sent to others, to lift a corner of the profound mystery that "happens" in the human person. In an address to families of the Neocatechumenal Way, John Paul II stressed that not only the individual members of a family, but the entire family has a missionary character. This mission unites the family in love.[43] In 1979, when I confided to him my perplexity at the idea of moving with my whole family to Rome, he said to me simply, "Think of it as a vocation! A mission!" The family that does not *"unleash the forces of good,* the source of which is found in Christ the Redeemer of man," and which *"every family unit needs to make . . . their own"*[44] will find its realization nowhere else.

The human person is born in the beauty of the gift that the mother makes to the father and the father to the mother. In their reciprocal self-giving, which is regulated by the logic of love, the human person finds a refuge and a defense. If this self-giving is lacking, the Church must speak with greater vehemence of the rights of children and the duties of parents and society in their regard. The child, too, should receive the same gift from the moment he is conceived. Man's beginnings can be unveiled, Hölderlin says, only by song. In today's society, the Church must sing the conception of the human person in the womb of his mother. Goethe understood this truth and showed it clearly in *Faust*.[45]

Unfortunately, today's Europe lacks great poets. For this reason, it

---

43. John Paul II, address to families of the Neocatechumenal Way movement, December 12, 1994: "The family as such has a missionary dimension. This dimension does not only touch the members individually, but involves all of them together, committing them as a community in a more profound bond of unity in charity and in a more lively missionary impetus."

44. John Paul II, *Letter to Families*, no. 23.

45. Cf. the scene in *Faust* in which the scientist Wagner, inspired by Mephistopheles, produces a person *in vitro* in his laboratory. Wagner's creation is called *homunculus*, "little man."

sees only phenomena that are the result of sophisticated calculations; it does not see what is. Contemporary Europeans live in Plato's cave, which is populated by slaves of opinion *(doxa)* who are far from the knowledge *(episteme)* of reality. They are unused to cultivating the earth that is the person, destined to the love in which other persons could dwell. They do not work for the revelation of truth that morally obligates society *(veritas est vir qui adest* — the truth is the man who is present). Work for the common good, that is, for the person of every human being, does not unite them. They do not help one another. Thus they are not in solidarity. Solidarity has a place in *cult*ure, not in "producture." In "producture," nothing is cultivated *(colo, colere, cultum* means "to cultivate the earth"). One wishes to produce everything, even the human being, his love and his freedom, according to circumstances and needs. Slaves of opinion believe that philosophy consists in calculating circumstances and phenomena. They reduce human acts to the *facere* that reveals not the person but the power of the logic of an unknown technical subject, to which modern man submits himself to the point of becoming an object of its making. Thus we enter into a phase of a new, technical "masterslave" dialectic. Man will not be able to free himself from it with his own ingenuity.

Karol Wojtyła analyzed the problem of solidarity in the final pages of *Person and Act*,[46] a few years before the founding of the Polish Solidarity movement. The first edition of this work appeared in 1969, but it was written a few years earlier. The monthly journal *Znak* had difficulties with the government censors, who did not want to allow these final pages to be published in the form of an article before the book came out. As the editor of the journal, I had chosen this fragment deliberately. It seemed to me that the issue of solidarity was of essential importance for the life of Polish society. On the one hand, there were authentic attitudes of solidarity in participation in work for the common good, as well as in opposition to the negation of this good on the part of the Communist regime. On the other hand, there was the problem of inauthentic attitudes of solidarity, such as conformity, which submits the person to the dominant negation of the common good, and the evasion by which he seeks to avoid being struck by the *praxis* of a regime that tramples the human person.

---

46. Karol Wojtyła, *Persona e atto* (Vatican City: Editrice Vaticana, 1980), chap. 7, pp. 316-30.

Marriage and the Family

These pages from *Person and Act* are even more pertinent today. In *Familiaris Consortio*, John Paul II writes that in our time the family is under attack on numerous fronts, always in the name of a freedom that is in reality uncontrolled free choice mixed with egoism. Consequently, the path is cut off that leads from marriage and the family to faith, hope, and love, where we find the sources of the person's moral duties. How can we remain in solidarity with marriages and families? How can we oppose those who deform and even negate these realities? How do we find the courage to reject conforming to the status quo or excusing ourselves from our duty to be an epiphany of the truth? (Post)modernity places us before these questions.

The author of *Radiation of Fatherhood* speaks of the difficult freedom that is love in terms that almost make us think we are hearing a personal confession:

> I later said to Him, complaining, "You could have left me in the sphere of fertility (I would somehow have reconciled myself to nature) without placing me in the depths of a fatherhood to which I am unequal! Why did You plant it in the soil of my soul? Was it not enough that You had it in Yourself? ...
>
> "Did You have to touch my thought with Your knowledge that means giving birth? Did You have to touch my will with the love that is fulfillment? I cannot give birth this way! In me love never fulfills itself. That is why You were disappointed in me."[47]

The playwright knows, however, that he is crying out against himself and against God, for he cries out against the "image" of God inscribed in his own person. Even now, God continues to work on this "image." Even now he asks the human person, "Give me a drink."

As far as I am aware, no pontiff has ever spoken so courageously about the sexually differentiated beauty of the body, thoughts, and actions of the human person, or of the person's sexually differentiated desire to experience the beauty of love. The beauty of the sexually differentiated love that unites man and woman shows us the way that leads to God — a way about which the Church had not said very much. The otherness of God's Transcendence is revealed in the differences that unite the human person with other persons, especially in sexual difference. The otherness

---

47. Wojtyła, *Radiation of Fatherhood*, pp. 336-37.

of woman speaks to man of God's Otherness, and the otherness of man speaks to woman of the same. Pascal observes that common minds, subjected to mathematical reason, do not notice differences.[48]

John Paul II defended man against this vulgar simplification of the human mind, especially when he stressed the fundamental importance of sexual difference for the development of the human person. He spoke of the beauty of woman with a delicate courage that he learned from Christ. Christ's most beautiful and profound dialogues were with women. He knew that because of their dedication to love, women see the truth of the human person better than men. They are more mature, so that they can say to the truth, *"Fiat mihi!"* Christ's priestly service of the Church-Bride formed John Paul II in this vision of woman and of her presence as mother and lady in the family, in society, and in the Church. We can never stress enough the importance of the role of women in Polish history, during times when our country was erased from the political map of Europe and the Polish people threatened with extinction.

* * *

Karol Wojtyła learned to love human love while preparing young people for marriage and accompanying them on their path of marriage and the family. He learned from them that when the husband says to his wife, "You are mine," he confesses that he belongs to her, not that he possesses her. These couples taught Wojtyła to contemplate the beauty of the human body, and they taught him its dignity. They told him that their desire to become one in the beauty of the truth that revealed itself in their beautiful bodies, thoughts, and actions aimed far: at the infinite. And that this desire served not so much the person's survival in time, but his continuation in eternity. It was these young couples, much more than theological and anthropological reflection, who showed Karol Wojtyła the truth that later would find expression in Paul VI's encyclical, *Humanae Vitae*.

Wojtyła's analysis of the word "mine" reveals the dignity and the moral character of the human person. The reciprocal belonging of persons to one another obligates them to behave adequately before one another. He who does not belong to anyone does not feel obligated to anything. The person who is not obligated is not reborn. He forgets that he

---

48. Blaise Pascal, *Pensées*, section 1, no. 7: "Ordinary persons find no difference between men."

is *naturus*. He lives according to the principle, "Do whatever you want!," that is, according to whatever his thoughtless freedom commands him. He does business with love, faith, and hope, selling his own freedom and trying to buy that of others. He fixes a price on the freedom that has no price, and treats himself and others accordingly.

The love of man and woman in marriage must not stop where it began. Love is like the dawn that sheds its light on everything in and around us. It begins in a precise here and now, but it is fulfilled infinitely further on, in the instant that is only coming, *advenire*. Husband and wife bear a shared responsibility for this instant. He who lives according to the principle, "Do whatever you want!," loses love. With it, he loses the awareness that he is always to be reborn in the relation of belonging to the other person, first of all in the belonging of man to woman and woman to man. Forgetting his own *natura*, he forgets natural laws, which have their origin here. In virtue of these laws, marriage, family, and Church cannot be reduced to keeping company with one another, with a limited responsibility that dissolves once its objectives are attained.

Contemplating the beauty of the body in the moral experience of the person's encounter with another person, John Paul II found not only a starting point for his anthropology, but also the place in which this anthropology joins with Christology (the Incarnation) and becomes an adequate anthropology. In *The Jeweler's Shop*, this adequate anthropology arises in Anna when she discerns in the face of the Bridegroom the face of her husband Stefan. Despite their mutual estrangement, she is joined to Stefan by their nuptial faiths, which form an indissoluble totality. Anna perseveres faithfully in love. She sees ever more clearly that love and forgiveness form such a unity that if forgiveness is banished, love is banished and vice versa. If this is how things are, then love must also be mercy.

Discerning the greatest beauty in the tortured body of Christ opened the young Wojtyła to an understanding of mercy. "Such beauty is called Mercy," says Brother Albert Chmielowski to Christ in the play *Our God's Brother*.[49] The truth of man, which reveals itself in the beauty called Mercy, cannot be that which seems to be strongest in a determinate moment. The truth that has its source in the eternal must become an ache in the person who orients himself by following his reflection in the flow

---

49. Karol Wojtyła, *Our God's Brother*, in *Collected Plays*, p. 227 (translation slightly altered).

of passing things. This is precisely what Adam tries to explain to Anna in *The Jeweler's Shop*, when he tells her:

> I could almost hear your soul. You were calling with despair for a love you do not have. You were looking for someone who would take you by the hand and hug you.
>
> Ah, Anna, how am I to prove to you that on the other side of all those loves which fill our lives — there is *Love!* The Bridegroom is coming down this street and walks every street! How am I to prove to you that you are the bride? One would now have to pierce a layer of your soul, as one pierces the layer of brushwood and soil when looking for a source of water in the green of a wood. You would then hear him speak: beloved, you do not know how deeply you are mine, how much you belong to my love and my suffering — because to love means to give life through death.[50]

Nostalgia for this merciful beauty gave a paschal form to John Paul II's desire for the Father's house — for his homeland. His desire was greater the more he saw lies all around him. His paschal desire formed his spiritual life above all in his final years. It was then that he uttered his most profound word about the human person and culture. When I told him this, he looked at me thoughtfully, as if he were searching for something behind me, and said, "I'm descending." I added, "into the depths, from where the words that reach us have a better and more beautiful sound."

Through a sorrowful nostalgia for that for which it is worth living and dying, a more-than-human force enters into man. Unfortunately, the time has come today about which Zarathustra warned us in Nietzsche's famous work: "The time is coming when man will no longer shoot the arrow of his longing beyond man, and the string of his bow will have forgotten how to whir!"[51] In times like this — in times of "producture," not culture — we need prophetic visions of the human person and prophetic decisions. Without these, the new evangelization will not be evangelization at all.

With prophetic decision, John Paul II called into being an Institute for Studies on Marriage and Family. He dreamed of a university that

---

50. Wojtyła, *Jeweler's Shop*, p. 64.
51. Friedrich Nietzsche, *Thus Spoke Zarathustra*, trans. Walter Kaufman (New York: Penguin, 1978), p. 17.

would be like a native land for people who sought the truth together, in a freedom governed by love. He dreamed of a university that would return to the origins of the university and to the Origin of man, as well as investigate his End. He dreamed of a university in which the truth of man would shine forth in the personal communion of students and teachers, who would contemplate it together. Confirmed in his experience that laypeople are more aware than clerics that the collapse of marriage and the family draws society and the Church in its wake, he called this Institute into existence without fearing the criticism he expected, which in fact came. It was voiced by the clergy, including a few bishops, but not by the laity. He thought this was entirely understandable. According to the author of *Person and Act*, acts bear witness to the person, not the opinions that circulate about him. "People have always and will always talk like this," he answered, when I repeated to him the criticism that rained down above all on the person he chose to carry out this prophetic decision, Msgr. Carlo Caffarra, the Institute's first president. "God will reward him for what he will have to put up with," the Pope added, with the clear certainty that anything else would not be possible.

John Paul II did not doubt that in marriage and the family there was something divine, which transfigured human weakness. For this reason, even the most gracious human words do not do justice to marriage and the family, just as hostile words do not damage them. For this reason, only the Word that God speaks does justice to marriage and the family. Precisely for this reason, an anthropology that lacks Christology is not equal to the truth of the human person. When the prophet speaks of man, he does not speak with his own strength but with the strength of the Word of the living God. This Word can lose a battle, but the final victory belongs to him alone. Yesterday's critics of the Pope's decision today have no doubt that the foundation of the Institute for Studies on Marriage and the Family was not a pure Wojtylian invention.

In *Crossing the Threshold of Hope*, John Paul II wrote,

> I had long been interested in *man as person*. . . . I was always more fascinated by man. While studying in the Faculty of Literature, man interested me inasmuch as he was a creator of language and a subject of literature; then, when I discovered my priestly vocation, man became the *central theme of my pastoral work*.
>
> By this point the war had ended and the controversies with Marxism were in full swing. In those years, my greatest involvement was

with young people who asked me questions, not so much about the existence of God, but rather *about how to live,* how to face and resolve problems of love and marriage, not to mention problems related to work.[52]

It was not easy to find solutions to these problems. The book *Love and Responsibility,* published in 1960,[53] was born from these conversations with young people who were preparing themselves for marriage and family life. Later, *Person and Act* would flow from the same source. Should not something similar happen in the Institute that bears John Paul II's name?

Doubtless the Nazi and Communist persecutions of the human person reinforced Wojtyła's conviction that the rejection of God ends in the rejection of man and vice versa. The reason that tramples on the divine truth present in man loses a healthy sense of direction and subjects itself to libertinism. Wojtyła saw how the reasoning of many intellectuals (with many theologians among them), especially in the West, found the difficult and often bloody struggle of simple people for a culture of man and for the worship of God, for the holiness of marriages and families and for the dignity of the human person, to be an obstacle. Their reason had made atheism and contempt for man into an intellectual game based on opportunism and ignorance. Is today's libertinism any different? It is doubtless more refined, but for this very reason isn't it more treacherous and cruel? But our hope is great, despite the evil that frightens us. Isn't it true that where evil rages, grace is all the more at work? The Church, who alone defends man and human love today, flourishes in people who are criticized, insulted, persecuted, and killed. She flourishes in people whom grace purifies of tares.[54] We have to know to ask for grace, that is, for the "gift of God." We have to ask the Holy Spirit, without whose breath

---

52. John Paul II, *Crossing the Threshold of Hope,* trans. Jenny McPhee and Martha McPhee (New York: Knopf, 1994), pp. 199-200.

53. A second edition was published in 1962, with the addition of a text on the theme of solidarity.

54. Cf. three books that treat this theme: (1) Ludmiła Grygiel, Stanisław Grygiel, and Przemysław Kwiatkowski, eds., *Bellezza e spiritualità dell'amore coniugale* (Siena: Cantagalli, 2009); (2) Stanisław Grygiel and Przemysław Kwiatkowski, eds., *L'amore e la sua regola: Karol Wojtyła e l'esperienza dell'"ambiente" di Cracovia,* Sentieri della verità 6 (Siena: Cantagalli, 2009); (3) Przemysław Kwiatkowski, *Lo Sposo passa per questa strada: La spiritualità coniugale nel pensiero di Karol Wojtyła,* Sentieri della verità 8 (Siena: Cantagalli, 2011).

man does not even know for what he should ask. The first person to show this truth to John Paul II was his father.

Man and woman work in love for the resurrection. Man is reborn in woman and woman in man. In order to be reborn, we first have to die in love. In love, the human person dies to himself to rise in the person he loves. Every day, through death, love leads him to a new life. The paschal path to that which fills our hope passes through marriage and the family, never through their substitutes. This paschal path leads to freedom. No "partnership" can take the place of marriage and the family. Unfortunately, in our day only the Church knows that "marriage and the family constitute one of the most precious of human values."[55] When people live from substitutes for these values, they cannot be in the world responsibly. Closed in their so-called freedom of choice, they constantly exchange "partners" because, seeing in them objects to be used, they do not find in any of them a "helper fit for them" (cf. Gen. 2:20). Their homelessness has an amoral character, since moral obligations arise from belonging to another person in a love that reaches eternity and thus the truth.

Self-knowledge and maturing toward one's own identity in the light of sexual difference do not necessarily mean living in marriage. And yet they do mean that even those who do not marry "for the sake of the kingdom of heaven" must see themselves in the light of this difference. If the question, "Who am I?" prescinds from sexual difference — if it is not posed in the light of the mystery of the bodily and spiritual union of the knowing subject with the known subject — it reduces friendships, marriages, families, as well as the Church who is present in these, to hypotheses. The functioning of these hypotheses is experimentally verified; they are modified or rejected according to the results. Questions asked in this way can provoke serious disturbances in the personal identity of those who pose them so abstractly.

The celibate person learns to "build bridges" that unite persons with other persons and ultimately with God. That is, he learns to be a *pontifex*, turning his gaze to the union of man and woman in "one flesh." If he does not do this, he is, as Plato said, a "common worker" *(homo faber)* who produces useful objects — beginning with man.[56] Norwid addresses

---

55. John Paul II, *Familiaris consortio*, apostolic exhortation on the role of the Christian family in the modern world, no. 1.

56. Plato, *Symposium* 203a. For "common worker," Plato uses the term *banausos*, a producer of objects.

with harsh words man's agitation, dominated by the will to success in the production of objects, marriage and family included: "Everywhere and always, slaves are slaves — if you give them wings, they will use these to sweep the streets."[57]

To live responsibly means to respond to the call that reaches us through other persons, through their bodies, thoughts, and actions. Our response to the call is inadequate; for this reason, we feel guilty. Only those who are solitary feel innocent, but nothing remains of their work, which contains neither love nor poetry. Yet in the deepest depths of human solitude is a fissure, through which God enters man. He enters as the Love that becomes the form of humanity. "You want me to love. You aim at me through a child, through a tiny daughter or son — and my resistance weakens. Nothing remains of the loneliness with which I resist You."[58] Generation, not solitude, is inscribed in the person's being. But generation, both according to the flesh and according to the spirit, involves pain. And we fear pain.

He who generates must help the one generated to be reborn continually. The father and mother educate the child, who also educates them because he helps them to be reborn. From the moment of conception, the child educates his parents more than they educate him. The child spiritually generates his parents. Parents must convert to their child, and the child to his parents. None of them is the property of the other. None of them is an object. Parents are not the owners of their children, nor children of their parents. Not even God possesses the human person. When we say that someone belongs to another person, we mean that he is oriented to this other. Every human being is ultimately oriented to God. "Before I formed you in the womb I knew you, and before you were born I consecrated you" (Jer. 1:5).

Parents must draw near with reverence to the mystery of the infant conceived in its mother's womb. A lack of this reverence desecrates all of us because it desecrates the act of creation on the part of God who alone is holy. He creates the human person and the world. The desecration of the Origin, of which the beauty of the person conceived is a memory, and of the End, which is manifested in the pain of conscience in people who do not receive the person sent to them with respect, negates the most pro-

---

57. Cyprian Norwid to Kleczkowski, September 1856, in *Pisma wszystkie*, vol. 8 (Warsaw: Państwowy Instytut Wydawniczy, 1971), p. 290.

58. Wojtyła, *Radiation of Fatherhood*, p. 338.

found content of history. And yet, "Can history ever flow against the current of conscience?"⁵⁹ Can man desecrate himself to such an extent that nothing remains of the beauty of the truth and the good safeguarded by conscience? Conscience reaches what reason cannot.

The beauty of truth and of love precedes the human person. It guides and educates him. Thanks to this beauty, he who is still "here" already dwells "over there." The fascination of beauty is the only way to educate the person for the Future. There is no other way to educate the human person, for he belongs to beauty. In other words, the family educates man. If the family creates the conditions in which, enraptured by the beauty of the true and the good, its members can follow what precedes and astonishes them, the family helps people to be reborn. Darkness falls in the person who is not enraptured by the beauty of the true and the good, such that he can no longer distinguish good from evil, truth from the lie, purity from impurity. Everything is indistinct in this darkness, in which the path is indicated step by step by "general opinion." The latter understands only the language of brute force and comfort.

In the Gospel, the scientifically minded Pharisees put Jesus to the test with the question, "Is it lawful to divorce one's wife for any cause?" (Matt. 19:3). They ask this question about marriage without being enraptured by the beauty of the love that unites man and woman. The question is abstract because they are moved by the contingent circumstances of their unions. They ask about marriage from outside the human person, not from his interior. A historical vision of marriage will always find some motive for one spouse to repudiate the other. Jesus sees marriage differently because he is enraptured by it. He does not see it in the light of the pressure of circumstances but in the light of the Origin and End. The scientifically minded do not concern themselves with these. They are not interested in the "prehistory" or the "post-history" of marriage. Hence the Pharisees' question reduces man to temporal things. It denies his subjectivity and thus also his capacity to be gift, that is, his capacity to entrust himself to another person forever. Jesus' answer immediately transfers their question about the historical "here" to the eternal "there." The Origin of the human person is known only by God and, according to Plato's *Timaeus*, "he of men who is the friend of God."⁶⁰ Jesus responds to

---

59. Karol Wojtyła, "Thinking My Country: Thinking My Country I Return to the Tree," in *Place Within*, p. 148.

60. Plato, *Timaeus* 53d, in *The Collected Dialogues of Plato*, trans. Benjamin Jowett,

the Pharisees as the one who knows what is in man, because he himself is man's Origin and End.

In his catecheses on marriage, John Paul II explains that "when Christ appeals to the beginning," he not only links this beginning to the mystery of creation. "He asks his interlocutors to go in some way beyond the boundary running in Genesis between the state of original innocence and the state of sinfulness that began with the original fall."[61] At this boundary, the "serpent" insinuates himself into man's relation with himself and with others, tempting him with the possibility of treating himself and others as something "good for food . . . a delight to the eyes, and . . . to be desired to make one wise" (Gen. 3:6). The "serpent" tempts us to entrust ourselves to circumstances.

At the boundary between original innocence and the original fall, man is ashamed. He senses that God seeks and sees him *(theós)*, yet he is willing to converse with the serpent. God sees him in every moment of the beauty of a love to which man is unequal. He sees him in the shame with which man clothes himself because he willed to forget love and, in it, his Origin and End. When the human person chooses metaphysical solitude in order not to hear the call to holiness and not to feel guilty at his own irresponsibility, he behaves shamelessly. Shameless people avoid those who are pure, for the latter's presence does not allow the former to forget their sin and reawakens their nostalgia for purity. The beauty he has abandoned, in whose light man is ashamed, makes him suffer grievously. Shame and grief prompt Adam to hide from God's gaze amid the trees of paradise. Adam wants to forget both his shame and his grief. This is also why Alcibiades hides himself in the presence of Socrates:

> Socrates is the only man in the world who has made me feel shame — ah, you didn't think I had it in me, did you? Yes, he makes me feel ashamed: I know perfectly well that I can't prove he's wrong when he tells me what I should do; yet, the moment I leave his side, I go back to my old ways: I cave in to my desire to please the crowd. My whole life has become one constant effort to escape from him and keep away,

---

ed. Edith Hamilton and Huntington Cairns (Princeton: Princeton University Press, 1980).

61. John Paul II, *Man and Woman He Created Them: A Theology of the Body*, trans. Michael Waldstein (Boston: Pauline Books and Media, 2006), p. 142.

but when I see him, I feel deeply ashamed, because I'm doing nothing about my way of life, though I have already agreed with him that I should. Sometimes, believe me, I think I would be happier if he were dead. And yet I know that if he dies I'll be even more miserable. I can't live with him, and I can't live without him. What *can* I do about him?[62]

The human person who hides from God's gaze has the same question: What can he do about God?

Friendship, marriage, the family, and the nation are neither concepts nor ideas. If they were, we could think of them differently. We could impose other forms on them and perhaps even live without them. Friendship, Aristotle writes, is "a virtue, or involves virtue; and also it is one of the most indispensable requirements of life. For no one would choose to live without friends, but possessing all other good things."[63] Narratives constructed on the basis of predicate propositions do not speak adequately of friendship, marriage, the family, and the nation. The only thing that can speak thus adequately *(benedicere)* is the song composed of joy and suffering, that is, existential propositions, the source of which can be found in "I AM WHO I AM."

This is why we may not leave marriage and the family in the hands of politicians and the masses on which they depend, for they manipulate these realities. Marriage and the family are governed by a divine element present in the human person — by the love that is freedom and the freedom that is love. In the confessional, the priest must bow before the mystery of this freedom and love, however stained they may be by man.

"*As a young priest I learned to love human love,*" John Paul II wrote. "This has been one of the fundamental themes of my priesthood — my ministry in the pulpit, in the confessional, and also in my writing. If one loves human love, there naturally arises the need to commit oneself completely to the service of 'fair love,' because love is fair, it is beautiful."[64]

Fr. Karol Wojtyła was reborn in the marriages and families he accompanied. He placed himself in their service so that their love might grow, opening itself to infinite Love and infinite Freedom. He behaved as if, next to them, his own person had to decrease. This is why criticisms claiming that John Paul II did not understand the contemporary human

---

62. Plato, *Symposium* 216b-c.
63. Aristotle, *Nicomachean Ethics* 1155a.
64. John Paul II, *Crossing the Threshold of Hope*, p. 123.

situation are infantile. He knew that man will be saved only by whatever beauty he manages to retain in himself, in his marriage and his family.

With a culture of love, he bore witness to the truth. With his culture, he entered into the culture of others. Together with them, he created living traditions of faith, hope, and love on earth. At the end of *The Jeweler's Shop*, Adam says,

> Sometimes human existence seems too short for love. At other times it is, however, the other way around: human love seems too short in relation to existence — or rather, too trivial. At any rate, every person has at his disposal an existence and a Love. The problem is: How to build a sensible structure from it? . . .
>
> That, too, is the ultimate sense of your lives:
>
> Teresa!
Andrew!
Anna!
Stefan!
>
> and yours:
>
> Monica!
Christopher![65]

And yet, *"Do not be afraid of the risks! God's strength is always far more powerful than your difficulties!"*[66]

---

65. Wojtyła, *Jeweler's Shop*, pp. 88-89.
66. John Paul II, *Letter to Families*, no. 18.

CHAPTER 5

Nation and State

How are things with Europe? In the mid-nineteenth century, Proudhon had no doubt that Europe, shattered by rationalism, was about to enter into a period of brute force and contempt for principles — a period of carousing. Twenty years later, in 1881, Cyprian Norwid drew the conclusions of lifelong experience in a letter to a friend: "Europe is an old, stupid drunkard who every few years massacres and kills without any civil or moral result.... It is incapable of building anything, stupid as a shoe, presumptuous, haughty and inconsiderate.... Ten million corpses, tears and money bags full of false coins."[1] Europe is governed by people who unite freedom not with truth, but with the possibility of making financial and State structures function according to rules of calculation. Functionaries of banks and of States behave as if they were slaves of the unforeseeable consequences of events provoked by circumstance or by their political and economic games. In Europe, such functionaries deprive man of freedom, for they think of everything except the dignity of the person, a dignity that comes not from an abundance of goods possessed, but from truth and love. Only a few enrich themselves, while Europe falls into cultural and moral misery.

John Paul II wrote that in the situation in which we find ourselves,

to a certain degree man does get lost; so too do preachers, catechists, teachers; and as a result, they no longer have the courage to preach the

---

1. Cyprian Norwid to Konstancji Górskiej, 1881, in *Pisma wszystkie*, vol. 10 (Warsaw: Państwowy Instytut Wydawniczy, 1971), p. 155.

threat of hell. And perhaps even those who listen to them have stopped being afraid of hell.

In fact, *people of our time have become insensitive to the Last Things.* On the one hand, *secularization and secularism* promote this insensitivity and lead to a consumer mentality oriented toward the enjoyment of earthly goods. On the other hand, the *"hells on earth"* created in this century which is now drawing to a close have also contributed to this insensitivity.[2]

Eschatology, and with it ultimate justice, have become foreign to us. As a result, nothing prevents us from manipulating earthly justice.[3] In *Centesimus Annus*, the Pope wrote of individual interests that overwhelm social interests, for when the human person does not know where he comes from and where he is going, he loses himself amid private goods and becomes an "idiot," in the original sense of this word. Society loses itself, too, as it subjects itself to state structures that develop toward an unknown future. The functionaries of these structures make people believe that they can understand themselves only by using soap, eating hot dogs, and relying on computers and tanks.

European politicians have bonds of friendship more with power as an object of possession than with wisdom. Consequently, they do not dwell in friendship with human beings. They do not dwell in the European landscape created by culture, that is, by the cultivation of values. Through this work of cultivation, the human person inserts himself into the tradition. He lives with generations of people who are present to him, even if most of them are a little farther away in the past or the future. Cultivating these values would introduce European politicians into the living tradition of the truth entrusted to their love. "The world of culture and art is called to build up the human person: to support him in his often tormented search for the true, the good and the beautiful. Culture and art are ... a marvelous synthesis, in which the highest values of existence, even in their contrasts between light and darkness, good and evil ... are ordered to a profound knowledge of man."[4] It is precisely this knowledge that is lacking to politicians today.

2. John Paul II, *Crossing the Threshold of Hope*, trans. Jenny McPhee and Martha McPhee (New York: Knopf, 1994), pp. 183.

3. John Paul II, *Crossing the Threshold of Hope*, p. 183.

4. John Paul II, address at the end of a concert in La Scala Theater, Milan, May 21, 1983.

Nation and State

The nation is born in a precise culture and in the poetry that expresses its foundation — in what Wojtyła calls "my country":

> When I think my Country —
> I express what I am, anchoring my roots.
> And this is what the heart tells,
> as if a hidden frontier ran from me to others,
> embracing us all within a past
> older than each of us;
> and from this past I emerge
> when I think my Country,
> I take her into me as a treasure,
> constantly wondering how to increase it,
> how to give a wider measure to that space
> it fills withal.[5]

One day in the 1970s, Cardinal Wojtyła ended a conversation with me about the fate of Polish émigrés by saying, "It is a great evil to uproot a man from his native land." In Rome, he said to the Polish diaspora, "Uprootedness represents a dangerous social ill." Uprootedness from one's country is a human spiritual drama, to which the psalmist gives voice in his lament, "By the waters of Babylon, there we sat down and wept, when we remembered Zion. On the willows there we hung up our lyres. For there our captors required of us songs, and our tormentors, mirth. . . . How shall we sing the Lord's song in a foreign land? If I forget you, Jerusalem, let my right hand wither!" (Ps. 136:1-5). European politicians uproot Europeans from their native land. They are thus politicians from Europe, but not European politicians.

So what is a "country"? Norwid writes, "If anyone had asked John III[6] as he marched on Vienna what a homeland was, he would have answered, 'It is that place where it is most pleasant to rest and to die, while one is continually disposed to live and to work wherever and whenever humanity is at stake.'"[7] One's country is one's native inheritance, the fruit of our forefathers' labor. Laboring with them, we attain the humanity that was

---

5. Karol Wojtyła, "Thinking My Country," in *The Place Within: The Poetry of John Paul II*, trans. Jerzy Peterkiewicz (New York: Random House, 1994), p. 141.
6. John III Sobieski, king of Poland and grand duke of Lithuania from 1674 to 1696.
7. Cyprian Norwid, "Co to jest ojczyzna?," in *Pisma wszystkie*, vol. 7 (Warsaw: Państwowy Instytut Wydawniczy 1973), p. 50.

entrusted to us. We attain it in the tradition of our ancestral dwelling, indicated by the name and surname we bear. Politicians who condemn citizens to emigrate spiritually from their homeland commit a spiritual crime against humanity. Hanna Malewska, a great moral and cultural figure in Poland under Communism, wrote, "The exiled man loses his gods, his home and his reason."[8]

John Paul II never felt that he was an exile. "Though I am outside my country, inasmuch as I am always in Rome and at times outside of Rome, I remain firmly in my country," he said to Poles in Nigeria.[9] He did not feel like an exile because the roots of his country reached into the eternity that is present in every time and place.

It is true that Poland is geographically located on the Vistula. But as a nation, it is a little farther away. On the Vistula, Poles, together with past and future generations, built a native home within the cultural and political sphere proper to the State. Yet this home transcends the State. It explains and justifies the State, whereas the reverse is not true. The State neither explains nor justifies the nation. The earthly patrimony of every nation, measurable from the point of view of time and space, is only an "image and likeness" of the promised inheritance toward which we journey, seeing and saluting it from afar. We rest and die "most pleasantly" only in this Promised Land. Our homeland's

> only frontier is the Coming which will join into one Body the struggles of conscience and the mysteries of history. . . .
>
> Let us not increase the shadow's measure. . . .
>
> We must not consent to weakness.[10]

We work for your and our freedom — it is for this that we fight and suffer, the Polish rebels wrote on their banners. Man offers his life in time for life in eternity, that is, for his native land.

It is helpful to recall here John Paul II's words in *Slavorum Apostoli*, lest we Poles be accused of an idiotic nationalism: "Separation from one's homeland, which God sometimes requires of those he has chosen, when accepted with faith in his promise is always a mysterious and fer-

---

8. Hanna Malewska, *Opowieść o siedmiu mędrcach* [The tale of seven Greek wise men] (Krakow: Znak, 2012), p. 107.

9. John Paul II, address to the Polish community in Lagos, February 16, 1982.

10. John Paul II, "Thinking My Country: Thinking My Country I Return to the Tree," in *Place Within*, p. 148.

tile pre-condition for the development and growth of the People of God on earth."[11] The Pope cited the call of Abraham (Gen. 12:1ff.), St. Paul's response to the request a Macedonian makes to him in a dream (Acts 16:9), as well as the work of Sts. Cyril and Methodius among the Slavs. In different ways, Karol Wojtyła and later John Paul II remembered that libertinism ends up deforming a politics that is not rooted in a homeland both "lost" and "promised." I was privileged to reflect with him at times on Norwid's words,

> To be national, we have to be super-national!
> To be human, we have to be
> More than human . . . to be two and yet one — why?[12]

Man and the nation exist "here," but their roots are "there," for this is their genealogy.

> My country's brow has not risen here;
> My flesh beyond Euphrates and the Flood,
> My spirit soars above Chaos,
>   I pay rent to the world.
> No nation fashioned or saved me,
> I recall eternity's span;
> David's key unlocked my lips,
>   Rome called me man.[13]

John Paul II showed us his own experience of his country, Poland, in a speech given in Paris to the UNESCO:

> I am the son of a nation that has lived through the greatest experiences of history. Its neighbors repeatedly condemned it to death, but it survived and remained itself. It retained its identity and national sovereignty, notwithstanding partitions and foreign occupation, not by relying on physical force, but relying solely on its culture. In a time of necessity, this culture proved itself to be a power stronger than all other forces. . . .

---

11. John Paul II, *Slavorum apostoli*, encyclical letter, June 2, 1985, no. 8.

12. Cyprian Norwid, "Rzecz o wolności słowa — II," in *Pisma wszystkie*, vol. 3 (Warsaw: Państwowy Instytut Wydawniczy, 1971), p. 569.

13. Cyprian Norwid, "My Country," in *The Burning Forest*, ed. and trans. Adam Czerniawski (Chester Springs, PA: Dufour Editions, 1988), p. 32.

There is a fundamental sovereignty of society that is manifest in the culture of a nation. This is the sovereignty by which man is at the same time supremely sovereign.... Protect culture as the apple of your eye, for the future of the great human family! Protect it! Do not allow this fundamental sovereignty to fall prey to political or economic interest. Do not allow it to become the victim of totalitarianism, imperialism, or hegemony, for which man does not count except as an object of domination and not as a subject of his own human existence.[14]

The State based on numbers rather than culture subjects the true, the good, and the beautiful to . . . numbers. Its numbers erupt into man's love, faith, and hope, his friendships, marriage, and family life, and destroy them.

John Paul II knew well the goodness and value of Polish culture, but he did not pretend not to see in the lives of Polish people what Wyspiański describes: "Vulgarity infects us . . . here mediocrity piles up in eyes, ears, and trickles into mouths."[15] In Warsaw, during a 1987 visit to Poland, the Pope cried out, "Poland, my country, you need evangelization just as other countries do!" It makes one think to know that at the time, many Poles thought that the Pope had more or less committed a gaffe during the state of emergency. The Polish people forgot too quickly that the call to freedom demands the courage to say "Yes!" every day to great values — values for which the universe is too small. The human person belongs to these values even in prison; even there, he is obliged to cultivate them.

It is easy to lose the eschatological vision of the separation of the weeds from the wheat, which John Paul II mentions in *Memory and Identity*.[16] This vision made many of us unbreakable. The Pope recalls a young priest from the West, a Flemish companion of his from his years of study after the war, who said to him, "'The Lord allowed the experience of such an evil as communism to affect you. . . . And why did he allow it? [. . .] We were spared this in the West, because perhaps we could not have withstood so great a trial. You, on the other hand, can take it."[17] Af-

---

14. John Paul II, speech to the United Nations Educational, Scientific and Cultural Organization (UNESCO), June 2, 1980, nos. 14-15.

15. Stanisław Wyspiański, *Le nozze: Dramma in tre atti*, trans. Silvano De Fanti (Bologna: CSEO, 1983), act 1, p. 105.

16. John Paul II, *Memory and Identity: Conversations at the Dawn of a Millennium* (New York: Rizzoli, 2005), p. 4.

17. John Paul II, *Memory and Identity*, p. 46 (bracketed ellipsis points mine).

ter Wojtyła became Pope, a European politician expressed the same idea to him, saying "'If Soviet communism comes to the West, we will not be able to defend ourselves. . . . There is no force strong enough to mobilize us for such a defense."[18] The Father "rich in mercy" — *dives in misericordia* (Eph. 2:4) — was able to draw a greater good out of evil, through the human mediation of the defenseless Polish people.[19] In the same book, the Pope says that when the ideologies of evil were developing in the first half of the twentieth century, the Divine Mercy — that is, the action of the Truth, who is God — began to reveal itself to the unknown person of Sister Faustina Kowalska in Płock, Wilno, and Krakow. If the Poles resisted these ideologies, it was only thanks to a Mercy infinitely greater than the evil that befell them.

Politics done in a cultural vacuum becomes a concern for the production of soap, hot dogs, and tanks. It serves neither man nor the nation that is born from him and forms a unity with him (which is why he belongs to it). The politicians of production do not know the meaning of the human person or the nation, for they do not know what culture is. They do not know that culture "is the first and fundamental proof of the nation's identity,"[20] and therefore also of human identity. After having liberated themselves from ethics, the functionaries of politics and economics construct history to the measure of their greed. Once it has reached a certain limit, this greed loses its strength, but it is powerless to stop the wheel it has set in motion. The history of greed unfolds in a cultural void in a manner both tragic and comical. Greed's "progress" is not progress, for it advances at a remove from the human person. Human "history abhors a vacuum, it fills it with accidents, cases . . . and misfortunes every fifteen years or so."[21]

Is it possible to engage in politics in a culture of love? With a concern for a progress that consists in human persons maturing in love? The confessor's advice to Adam in *Our God's Brother*, "Let yourself be molded by love,"[22] also applies to politicians. They, too, are called to exercise that

---

18. John Paul II, *Memory and Identity*, p. 48 (ellipsis points original).

19. Cf. John Paul II, *Memory and Identity*, p. 50.

20. John Paul II, address to the 169th Plenary Assembly of the Polish Episcopal Conference, Częstochowa, June 5, 1979, no. 4.

21. Cyprian Norwid to Marian Sokołowski, January 27, 1864, in *Pisma wszystkie*, vol. 9 (Warsaw: Państwowy Instytut Wydawniczy, 1971), p. 125.

22. Karol Wojtyła, *Our God's Brother*, in *The Collected Plays and Writings on Theater*, trans. Boleslaw Taborski (Berkeley: University of California Press, 1987), p. 210.

care for the common good, that is, for the human person, which is called love. The love that fills a person's will has its roots in his homeland. A politics separated from this homeland does not create culture because, as Thomas Aquinas says, it does not live from reason and art. This kind of politics is performed far from the beauty of the true and the good.

The nation creates culture. The State, for its part, creates culture to the extent that it favors the nation and provides conditions favorable to love and work. Left to itself, the State constructs a technical civilization that becomes a curse, if not for the culture, then for the person and the nation. In a technical civilization, neither the person nor the nation are reborn. The nation can lose its State, but if it has the courage to remain in its own culture, sooner or later it will appear again as a State on the map of the world. This is what happened with both Poland and Israel. The State does not exhaust the interior content of persons and their nations. When the State is not aware of this, it behaves inhumanly. It subjects the sacred *intimum* of the human person, which is his moral conscience, to political decisions.[23] What the Polish king Sigismund Augustus said to the representatives of the Polish people is worth remembering: "I am not the king of your consciences."

The State is not the owner of its citizens. *They* rather possess *it*. The State does not constitute interpersonal communion, but must create the space for it. When it does create this space, it is a great State. It must not meddle in the mystery of human birth or death, or the mystery of a person's choice of this or that mode of life. The State must simply regulate its citizens' *facere* so as to protect and aid the development of their *esse* and *agere*. That is, the State must protect and aid its citizens' love and knowledge of the beautiful truth, and of the good that is just as beautiful. The person's "I am" (*esse*), and the love and knowledge (*agere*) that come to be in this "I am," transcend the State. The person's love and knowledge constitute the State's transcendence; all the State's efforts should be oriented to this. The State is secondary with respect to persons and the forms of interpersonal communion, for example marriage and the family, in which human beings realize themselves as persons. State laws that are not rooted in the person and his duties, which are derived from his belonging to other persons, are morally and culturally invalid. Their only "validity" is founded on police power.

---

23. Cf. Second Vatican Council, Pastoral Constitution on the Church in the Modern World, *Gaudium et spes*, December 7, 1965, no. 16: "*Conscientia est nucleus secretissimus atque sacrarium hominis.*" ["Conscience is the most secret core and sanctuary of a man."]

Nation and State

A politics whose agents do not reveal themselves (cf. *Person and Act*) is an anthropology of lies. It degenerates into a corrupt seeking of one's own advantage, into a politics of "idiots." The politician ought to be an artist, like a shoemaker who makes his shoes out of love, so that the shoes bring out women's beauty. The politician who is an artist brings out the personal beauty of the citizens he serves. Only he does justice to them. Every form of justice demands a love of the truth that reveals itself in persons who are present *(vir qui ad est)*. Without love, justice would be injustice. Plato was right when he said that it is the just, that is, the friends of the truth *(filosofia)* — or, if you will, the lovers of truth — who govern society. The greatest Athenian politician, Socrates, did not play political games. He simply helped people to discern the truth present within themselves. In this way, Socrates laid the foundations for just governance *(politeia)* in the State *(polis)*. To the judges who condemned him to death, he said, "I believe that I'm one of a few Athenians — so as not to say I'm the only one, but the only one among our contemporaries — to take up the true political craft and practice the true politics."[24]

Socrates did not aspire to power. All he did was show the citizens that they were living in appearances of the true and the good, instead of seeking what was genuinely true and good so that their lives might have meaning and value. Great politics can be identified not with maintaining power at whatever the cost, but with a preoccupation for the common good, that is, for the person who seeks the truth to which he belongs. Such a preoccupation often leads to the neglect of one's own goods or even to the loss of one's life.

A politician with a firm grasp on power who thinks of nothing else is not a politician in the profound sense of the word. Socrates chose a fate that left him no "leisure to engage in public affairs"[25] and made him despised and abandoned by almost all. He held that this "private" concern for the common good of the State or city *(polis)* was "a service to the god" *(he tou theou latreia,* and also *he to theo hyperesia)*.[26] Devoted to this service, he preached the difficult but beautiful truth to all. He flattered no one. In the *Gorgias*, he says to Callicles, "Now, please describe for me precisely the type of care for the city to which you are calling me. Is it that of striving valiantly with the Athenians to make them as good as possible,

---

24. Plato, *Gorgias* 521d.
25. Plato, *Apology* 23c and 30a.
26. Plato, *Apology* 23c and 30a.

like a doctor, or is it like one ready to serve them and to associate with them for their gratification?"[27] An immature society judges great politicians in the way a sick child judges a doctor who does not give him candy and who, as in Plato's dialogue, is accused by a cook.[28] The Athenian democracy killed Socrates with a majority of votes, but it was he, not they, who conquered.

No "illegitimate students" should take up politics, understood as acting from within a friendship with wisdom.[29] Whoever chooses his friends or his rulers must keep in mind whom he is choosing: "When either a city or an individual doesn't know how to do this [i.e., distinguish the legitimate from the illegitimate], it unwittingly employs the lame and illegitimate as friends or rulers."[30] The wise politician labors in politics "for the city's sake, not as if he were doing something fine, but rather something that has to be done."[31] Thus those who lack principles should not take up politics, and society should not entrust such people with its own fate. They unbind politics from truth and transform it into something absolute. They make it dissolute. A dissolute politics, that is, a politics that has been made *sacrum*, is founded on the principle professed by the wicked in the book of Wisdom: "Let our might be our law of right, for what is weak proves itself to be useless" (Wisd. 2:11). A dissolute politics compels people to be rooted in the fashions of the moment, or more precisely, in their effectiveness and usefulness. These qualities are held to be the highest good, and corrupt society. A dissolute politics cannot tolerate those who unite themselves to reality, taking root in its truth with the help of Jewish prophecy and Greek friendship with wisdom. A dissolute politics hates with an ever-growing hatred those who adore the Truth nailed to the cross.

Wise men — for we are speaking of wise men — attach their political plow to ideal and enduring values, without which the life that is "being a person" would be extinguished in the human being. "I will tell you in truth," writes Norwid. "The fate of the nations/And the events of humanity, the world and heaven . . ./Everything — receives life from the Ideal."[32] John Paul II meant precisely this when, in response to a journal-

---

27. Plato, *Gorgias* 521a.
28. Plato, *Gorgias* 521d-e.
29. Plato, *Republic* 7.535c.
30. Plato, *Republic* 536a.
31. Plato, *Republic* 540b.
32. Cyprian Norwid, "W pracowni Guyskiego," in *Pisma wszystkie*, vol. 2 (Warsaw: Państwowy Instytut Wydawnicz, 1971), p. 194.

ist's question about the formation of politicians, he said, "To be a Christian, one has to be holy. To be a Christian politician, one has to be all the more holy."[33]

Unfortunately, most politicians do not look to the starry heavens to seek support for themselves. Since they are not attached to the stars, they do not even manage to be particularly pragmatic. They can't manage to till the fields within the borders that were meant for them. Since they don't know where they come from, they don't know what their political action should aim for. They dance in time to music played by others more powerful than they. So it is not surprising that instead of statesmen, we have many crude politicians who, because they are unable to govern society, know only how to manipulate the masses. Together with crude journalists, they manipulate society into ever-greater stupidity. Since they know how to govern only an imaginary society, they administer "the shades" of Plato's cave.

We have forgotten that we are called to holiness. Thus we have been reduced to such a state that anyone can be a politician — not so unlike Caligula, who made his horse a senator. Politicians who are like Caligula's horse do not understand King Solomon's prayer upon ascending the throne: "Give thy servant therefore an understanding mind to govern thy people, that I may discern between good and evil" (1 Kings 3:9). For these horse-like politicians, what is indispensable is not the *ars gubernandi* but the *ars administrandi*. Norwid called States administered by such politicians a negation of that moral unity, without which "political parties are like gangs or polemical camps, whose fire is discord and whose reality is the smoke of words."[34] An administrator of objects needs to know only a few empty words, with which he can direct the mass of individuals. Where are they going? Straight ahead, right to their nose.

John Paul II was aware that the art of governing, *ars gubernandi*, is a spiritual event. He understood politics and economics through the question, "What is man?" "To understand man, we must enter into the light of the mystery. To understand the nation, we must go to its sanctuary."[35] Whoever does not enter into the light of the mystery of the human person

---

33. John Paul II, remarks given on a flight to Santo Domingo, Dominican Republic. Cf. *L'osservatore romano*, October 11, 1992.

34. Cyprian Norwid, "Głos niedawno do wychodźstwa polskiego przybyłego artysty," in *Pisma wszystkie*, vol. 7, p. 8.

35. Karol Wojtyła, "Homilia do artystów, poetów, pisarzy," in *Kazania 1967-1978* (Krakow: Znak, 1979), p. 478.

will not understand man, and whoever does not go to the nation's "sanctuary" will not understand the society in which that person lives. We must be on guard against politicians who have hung signs in their office saying, "It's the economy, stupid!" We can trust only those politicians and economists whose political and economic decisions are guided by a culture born "in the light of the mystery." Jean Monnet[36] said that if he could form the European Union all over again, he would have begun not with the European Coal and Steel Community, but with the community of culture.

Culture always has a religious character. At the basis of the error called a "vicious cycle," in which politics and economics justify one another with themselves, we find atheism, which liberates politics and economics from ethics by separating them from culture. In doing so, it condemns politics and economics to making up political actions according to the caprice of a "continually negating" spirit.[37] The exclusion of Transcendence from a society's life and culture leads to totalitarianism. The content and form of this totalitarianism depend on that beside which the desire of the restless human heart has halted. Every totalitarianism raises the lie to the dignity of the truth, and evil to the dignity of the good. Some forms of totalitarianism do this with brutality (I would call these "hard totalitarianism"), and some with blandness (I would call this "soft totalitarianism"). But all the forms use fear as a principle of domination over the people. Even the totalitarianism of money and pleasure that now dominates the Western world does not renounce fear. Fear allows it to administer people in such a way as to create a new man and a new society. John Paul II saw what was not obvious to many: the creation of this new man and new society began with the separation of the act of conjugal love from generation, in the proper sense of the word — from the new man in both the spiritual and the biological sense. So it is not surprising that he spoke a firm "No!" to this impermissible action.

Faithful to the Church's Tradition, this Pope proclaimed a social doctrine based not on the *facere* of ecclesiastical politics but on the law of love *(agere)*, which alone is able to conquer fear and illegality. He judged the social politics of States with a gaze fixed on the dignity of the person, a dignity that is visible only to those who live in the order of love *(ordo amoris)*. By reason of his personal dignity, which the State did not give

---

36. A French political economist and diplomat who was one of the architects of the European Union.

37. Cf. Goethe, *Faust*, v. 1340.

Nation and State

him, man transcends the State. The State is for man and his dignity (cf. *Centesimus Annus*). Man is older than the State. Inasmuch as the Church's social doctrine points to the source of the human being's personal dignity, it cannot be reduced to moral rules of behavior that govern human coexistence.

John Paul II encouraged laypeople to participate in the political life of their country. But he also reminded them that as soon as they entered politics, they had to integrate their political activities with their spiritual life so that the justice they pursued would be justice rendered to the human person and not to fashionable opinions about him. If they fell short of the human person, they would hear in their interior the cry of the prophet Isaiah: "How the faithful city has become a harlot, she that was full of justice! Righteousness lodged in her, but now murderers. Your silver has become dross, your wine mixed with water. Your princes are rebels and companions of thieves. Every one loves a bribe and runs after gifts" (Isa. 1:21-23).

When a politician sets out to serve society, he must keep before his eyes the image of the Good Samaritan. Moved with compassion for the man beaten and left by thieves, the Samaritan stopped and tended to him, putting aside the business to which he had to attend in Jericho. John Paul II grieved that politicians behaved like the priest and the Levite of the parable rather than like the Samaritan. The degree to which the negation of the gift has progressed in the world, as well as the libertinism that is called freedom, worried the Pope. It pained him how much Europe had ceased to be a society, inasmuch as its citizens were not educated to know the gift and to be a gift for one another. People who do not live as a gift do not live as persons. They form a mass of individuals who struggle to possess ever more money. This in turn leads them to the idolatrous adoration of the golden calf and thus to corruption. In order to defend the Israelites from the idolatry that was corrupting them, Moses led them out of Egypt into the desert, where "having" decreased and "being" increased. In the desert, one adores Him who alone is. Idolaters behave like Baron Münhausen, who tried to pull himself out of a bog by his hair.

"Europe is not closed and isolated," John Paul II said. "It took shape in an encounter with other peoples, cultures and civilizations. . . . Other countries and continents expect from her courageous initiatives that are indispensable for building a more just and fraternal world."[38] Geograph-

---

38. John Paul II, message to Cardinal M. Vlk on the occasion of the Plenary Session of the European Bishops' Conferences, October 16, 2000.

ically, Europe obviously "extends from the Atlantic to the Urals, from the North Sea to the Mediterranean."[39] Yet, as the Pope clarified a few years later while speaking to the Polish diplomatic corps, if we wish to see the dawn of "a new and undivided Europe," we need "a vision of Europe from the East to the West as a spiritual-material unity.... Despite the extraordinary and surprising political dimension of events, we need to think of a future Europe also as a 'continent of culture.'"[40]

Europe is not so much a continent as an event. It is a spiritual and therefore a cultural event, which takes place in a particular place and time but is not identified with this place and time. This event takes place in people who are "here," but who greet from afar that which is found "there" and journey toward it (cf. Heb. 11:13). Europe is accomplished in persons; it is rooted in the Transcendence that seduced it, like Zeus who took on the form of the bull to ravish Europa, the daughter of the king of Tyre.

Europe "happens" in people's pilgrimage in faith and hope toward the land of the true and the good, which is promised by every fragment of beauty on this earth. Europe is a great exodus from every momentary situation to the Transcendence that seduces it. It can say with Jeremiah, "O Lord, thou hast deceived me, and I was deceived; thou art stronger than I, and thou hast prevailed" (Jer. 20:7). Europe ascends the hill where it strikes root in the earth under the cross. It ascends the Areopagus, where it put down roots in the Greek desire for truth — a desire that gave form to Athens' thought (cf. Acts 17:23). Following the requirements of a social order, it put down roots in Rome's juridical order, which still serves as the fundamental structure of European institutions. Europe journeys toward its ideal, but this ideal only shines like the dawn in those who build it up.

"Europe owes much to Christianity. But Christianity also has many reasons to thank Europe."[41] A few years before making this statement, John Paul II said, "The Church and Europe are two realities that are intimately bound in their being and their destiny."[42] And again, "How impoverished European culture would have been without its Christian inspiration!"[43]

---

39. John Paul II, homily for the celebration of vespers of Europe, Vienna, Austria, September 10, 1983.

40. John Paul II, speech to the Diplomatic Corps of Poland, Warsaw, June 8, 1991.

41. John Paul II, speech on his departure from Vienna airport, June 21, 1998.

42. John Paul II, address to participants in the fifth symposium of the Council of the European Bishops' Conferences, October 5, 1982.

43. John Paul II, address to the Polish Parliament, Warsaw, June 11, 1999.

Nation and State

Every spiritual event — and therefore also the event that is Europe — demands something more than knowing how to produce things that are useful for sustaining life on earth. Spiritual events transcend themselves. It is in them that man is reborn. Precisely for this reason, everything that closes Europe into its geographical and political-economic borders leads to destruction. Europe is bigger. Its borders must be sought within the European man or woman, whose heart and character are marked by truth and the love of freedom. These borders must defend nations and the families out of which they are formed. They must defend the common good of families and nations at times even against their own States, and against the bureaucratic administration that today bears the name of the European Union. When John Paul II affirmed that "a faith that does not become culture is a faith that has not been fully received or reflected, and not faithfully lived,"[44] he had in mind laborious love and equally laborious hope. In this love and hope are revealed the freedom that Europe was born in Greece to defend. This freedom is fulfilled on Golgotha.

Europe matures in the people who dwell in it not when they produce useful and comfortable objects, but when they seek the only thing without which man may live comfortably, but not beautifully or wisely. In the terms of classical philosophy, Europe "happens" more in *actio immanens* than in *actio transiens*. In *actio immanens*, that is, in love and knowledge, the human person journeys toward the values that decide his greatness and dignity. These values also decide the greatness of Europe. "The dignity of the person, the sacred character of life, the central role of the family, the importance of education, the freedom to think, to speak and to profess one's own convictions or religion . . . the concept of work as a sharing in the Creator's own work, the authority of the State, itself governed by law and reason," are *"values belong[ing] to the cultural treasure of Europe."*[45]

The *oikos*, the home or dwelling place, that is Europe cannot be identified with any ideology. Europe is a field (in Greek, *nomós*). Its borders are traced out by a laborious and solidary presence in it of a single person for all the others, and an equally solidary and laborious presence of all persons for that single person, when he asks, "Give me a drink." The truth revealed in this field *(nomós)* that is Europe, expresses itself in a custom

---

44. John Paul II, address to participants in the National Congress of the Ecclesial Movement for Cultural Commitment, January 16, 1982.

45. John Paul II, address at a meeting with the Swedish university community, Uppsala, June 9, 1989, no. 4.

and a law *(nómos)* that defines how this dwelling place is governed: the European *oikonomia*. Europe ceases to be that which it should be when the law of its *oikonomia* is no longer the person's presence to another person. When this happens, the European *oikouméne* becomes a conflict, in which the dwelling places of the mighty prevail over those of the weak. It is the latter who know what the person and his dwelling place are. They know the meaning of "economy" and *ekumenia*. Such things can be known only by those who do not seek others' defeat.

John Paul II regarded Europe as a people on pilgrimage toward Golgotha and going up to the Areopagus, where faith in Beauty crucified on a hill outside Jerusalem "incarnated" itself for the first time in a non-Jewish culture. On Golgotha, Christ continues to accomplish the ultimate and supreme act of love that reveals the truth of man; he transforms the Greek culture *(cultura,* or cultivation) of the human person's search for the beautiful and the good *(kalokagathía),* drawing it into the paschal mystery. Entrustment to Christ and the worship *(cultus)* of his Person give form to Europe's identity. With its help, other peoples on other continents matured and continue to mature in being themselves.

"Modern Western European countries have arrived at a stage which could be defined as 'post-identity.'"[46] In other words, in those countries, people have forgotten heaven and so also forget the earth — *nomós* and *nómos*. They stop seeking in it the sources that are indispensable to the spiritual life. Europe's aversion to Easter would have to become an aversion to Europe itself.

"Poland is part of Europe."[47] For this reason, it, too, should contribute to improving the cultivation of the European field or *nomós*. The "two lungs" with which Europe breathes — an expression John Paul II borrowed from the Russian poet Wiaceslaw Ivanow — meet in Poland. Only God can restore to these lungs their broken unity. Man can destroy the gift, but he cannot remake it. A reconstituted gift will never be a gift. If Europe should once more receive the gift of the Church's unity, the East will help the West to understand that the person will never manage to be rooted in his own thoughts and opinions, as Enlightenment thinkers advise. And the West will help the East to understand that the human person transcends the State and its politics.

John Paul II stressed that these two anthropological errors, of the

---

46. John Paul II, *Memory and Identity*, p. 86.
47. John Paul II, *Memory and Identity*, p. 91.

West and of the East, are a single error into which both Marxism and liberalism fall. Both of these systems led European societies to believe that the true and the good are products of the individual's reason and will, and that to keep afloat, the individual can do nothing but entrust himself to the effectiveness of his own inventions and choices. The exhibition of a human being badly thought of and treated as Europe's "new man" is an attempt to construct a ruthlessly inhuman new Europe.

John Paul II proclaimed no social doctrine beyond the doctrine that is the human person and thus also his culture. Together with the Church, he looked at society and judged its successes according to how it deepened the question of the human person in the circumstances in which it finds itself. The Pope bore witness to the faith of the Church, which deepens the truth of man with a contemplative question posed through the God-man to the Trinitarian society of Persons in God. This truth already reveals itself prophetically in the question. The Church's social doctrine cannot be identified with any political or economic system, for it transcends these. If I may put it thus, it points to a star or ideal, from which these systems must take their orientation. The people who live in these systems give to Caesar the coins that bear his image. But when they enter into the *sacrum*, that is, the temple that they themselves are as persons — and they should enter this in all their thoughts and actions — they exchange these coins for the currency of the holy space of their persons. The Jews exchanged Caesar's coins the moment they entered the Temple, since within this space one could pay only with money that was worthy of the holy place. We might say that they could pay only with transfigured coins. In other words, the question about man must transfigure the questions about political and economic systems according to the "interior discipline of the gift," which these systems do not know. At best, systems are pocket flashlights. Thus they need ideals or "stars," so that "everything receives its life from the Ideal" (Norwid).

The Church's social doctrine does not tell us what system the State ought to follow or which party ought to hold power. The Church simply reminds us that every political system must allow itself to be "formed by love," since it must serve the human person formed by love. The anthropological question, "Who is man?," precedes the political and economic questions about his dwelling place, *oikós*. Wherever all this takes place in inverse order, tyrannies of the economic or political majorities or tyrannies of rebellious minorities give form to the State. It is Mephistopheles of Goethe's *Faust* who makes use of this conflict between components ("classes") that reject one another. But even Mephistopheles answers the question "Who am I?" with "I am a part of the power that always wills evil and yet does the good, I am the spirit that always negates."[48] The evil that negates the good wounds the human person, and yet even in wounding him it bears witness to the truth and the goodness of his being. Even evil is epiphanic, in a certain sense; there would be no evil if there were no good. The truth and the good cannot be conquered. Mephistopheles, who knows this, is gripped by despair. But in man, this knowledge can rekindle hope.

Confronted with the rejection of the presence of Christ's Person and the negation of the human person's presence in social and political life, John Paul II said, "No! We cannot continue to live negating Christ and man!" In Warsaw during his first papal pilgrimage to Poland, he said this with a prayer that was like a challenge to God: "Let your Spirit descend and renew the face of the earth, the face of this land."[49] In a completely nonpolitical way, he changed politics, shifting it to a higher level. He shifted it "there," where the human person and society — "here" shattered into meaningless fragments — are recomposed in a new and beautiful whole. He shifted it under the cross. For this Pope, the cross, which he called the "root and meaning of life," is the first and ultimate place of the struggle for man. On the cross, we see who man is for God and who God is for man. The cross thus teaches us to govern our being and the being of society (the *nomós* of man and the *nomós* of society). The politician comes here, both to the foot of the cross and to the Aereopagus, to learn what it means to be a statesman and not merely a politician.

Europe is born in the "No!" the Greeks heroically uttered against the Persian invasion, and in the prophetic "Yes!" with which the Jewish people responded to the Most High God. When Europe forgets the Greek "No!" and the Jewish "Yes!," it falls prey to totalitarianism. The latter includes today's libertinism, which allows individuals to do everything they think or desire. Thus, in Europe, words function as if their content depended on the reasoning of individuals, which in turn is identified with their will. The Bible strongly affirms that when prophetic vision is lacking, the people lose every restraint, and blessed is he who observes the law (cf. Prov. 29:18). The drama of today's Europe has its origins in the lack of a prophetic vision of the human person and society. In other words, it has

---

48. Goethe, *Faust*, vv. 1337-38, 1340.
49. John Paul II, homily for Holy Mass, Victory Square, Warsaw, June 2, 1979.

its origins in a failure to see the truth to which both the human person and society belong. All those who do not look on themselves and society in the light of a guiding star or ideal do not see this. They do not observe the Law. John Paul II said to the participants of the 1982 Symposium for European Bishops, "Today Europe is crisscrossed by currents, ideologies and ambitions that desire to be extraneous to the faith, even if they are not directly opposed to Christianity.... The crises of European man are the crisis of Christian man. The crises of European culture are crises of Christian culture."[50]

The lack of prophecy deforms reason, depriving it of its capacity to distinguish between the truth and evil. The human person is no longer kept from losing the path of life. Prophecy always points to the cross, where man sees how things are with himself and with the world. Even Plato said that the truly just man would be mocked and killed. Reason, prophecy, and the cross must be fundamental moments in the new evangelization of Europe and the world. In a poem written almost on the first day he was elected Pope, Karol Wojtyła affirmed this in words he placed on the lips of the martyr-bishop of Krakow, killed by King Boleslas:

> Stanislas may have thought: my word will hurt you
> and convert,
> you will come as a penitent to the cathedral gate,
> emaciated by fasting, enlightened by a voice within,
> . . . .
> If the word did not convert you, the blood will.
> . . . .
> A sword falls on the soil of our freedom.
> Blood falls on the soil of our freedom.[51]

The prophetic reason that stands at the foot of the cross does not engage in politics, but it does show politics the direction in which the restless human heart tends. An ecclesial reason that participates in the Church's faith in God crucified as well as in man who stands at the foot of the cross, defends the human person and society. It points to the cross through which we must pass like a door to a new life. The Church engages

---

50. John Paul II, address to participants in the fifth symposium of the Council of the European Bishops' Conferences, October 5, 1982.

51. Karol Wojtyła, "Stanislas," in *Place Within*, pp. 181-82.

in no other politics, even if the bureaucrats of the European Union do not wish to acknowledge this.

The Pope said "Yes!" to the European Union, but at the same time he said "No!" to those who destroy the values that make it grow. They treat Europe as if it were no different from a broken clay pot held together by the wire of ever new treaties calculated by bankers, financiers, and politicians. A Union that imposes on nations and their States ideological answers to the *"magna questio"* is an anti-cultural creation. John Paul II said "Yes!" to the culture of the human person, so that a stronger enemy hand might not shatter Europe into fragments lacking importance and meaning. But he said "No!" to an artificial Union, constructed for economic interests and for bureaucrats. The latter look at these interests as at a subject who must be served. Patched clay pots do not have a great future before them. John Paul II said "Yes!" to heroic thought and life, that is, to the spirit of knighthood that seeks and defends the truth. Today Europe is weak, since its thought and will are weak. In a homily delivered in Warsaw on June 9, 1991, during the Mass for the beatification of Fr. Rafal Chyliński, the Pope said to the Polish people,

> The freedom for which Christ sets us free has been given . . . not so that we should waste it, but . . . live it and transmit it to others! We have to begin from this truth about Europe. And at the same time we have to realize . . . that Christ as the artisan of the European spirit, as the artisan of the freedom that has its salvific roots in him, was bracketed. Another European mentality began to be formed, which we can express in this sentence: "We think and live as if God did not exist." Of course, if Christ was bracketed and perhaps completely eliminated, God, too, would no longer exist. . . . This is the truth about man, the truth about European man. And we Poles cannot betray this truth about man! This is why we are always speaking of a new evangelization.[52]

At the beginning of the 1960s, he said to the circle of people that had grown around the weekly *Tygodnik Powszechny* and the monthly journal *Znak* in Krakow, "Creating works of Christian culture means not only confessing the faith and bearing witness, but also being an apostle. . . .

---

52. John Paul II, homily at Mass for the beatification of Rafal Chyliński, Warsaw, June 9, 1991.

Truth is the foundation of culture — and we have to guard this foundation as if it were one of our eyes."[53]

John Paul II saw Poland as a place from which the breath of the Holy Spirit could reach the whole of Europe. Recalling his first papal visit to his homeland in a homily delivered at Gniezno in 1997, during a Mass commemorating the 1,000th anniversary of the martyrdom of St. Adalbert, he said,

> From this place there flowed forth at that time the power and strength of the Holy Spirit. Here reflection on the new evangelization began to take shape in concrete terms. . . . The wall which divided Europe collapsed. . . . A half century of separation ended, for which millions of people living in Central and Eastern Europe had paid a terrible price. . . .
>
> . . . *There will be no European unity until it is based on unity of the spirit.* This most profound basis of unity was brought to Europe and consolidated down the centuries by Christianity with its Gospel, with its understanding of man and with its contribution to the development of the history of peoples and nations. This does not signify a desire to appropriate history. For the history of Europe is a great river into which many tributaries flow, and the variety of traditions and cultures which shape it is its great treasure. The foundations of the identity of Europe are built on Christianity. And its present lack of spiritual unity arises principally from the crisis of this Christian self-awareness.[54]

Human and Christian identity demands to be defined more profoundly and much more adequately every day, but this is not the job of the State. The State has no right to do this. The Christian himself has to do this. The State ought merely to help him. In other words, a State that wants to be the sole educator of its people is an evil State. It can turn him into a "correct citizen," but this is not enough to be a good man. We have to demand that the State place no obstacles before the love that forms the human person in marriage, the family, and friendship. Only a good person — that is, a person who has been formed by love — can be a good citizen. The State destroys itself when it places its citizens in the dilemma of having to be first correct citizens and only afterward good people; or when its citizens,

---

53. Karol Wojtyła, "Chrześcijanin a kultura," *Znak* 16, no. 10 = 124 (1964): 1156.
54. John Paul II, homily at Mass for the one-thousand-year anniversary of the martyrdom of St. Adalbert, Gniezno, June 3, 1997, nos. 3-4.

abused by political correctness, are afraid to be good people first. Such a State loses itself in the noise of decisions made in parliamentary shows under the pressure of passing circumstances. The functionaries of an exhibitionist politics do not want to keep in mind the words of St. Augustine: "The symbol of the holy mystery that you have all received together and that today you have recited one by one, are the words on which the faith of Mother Church is firmly built above the stable foundation that is Christ the Lord. You have received it and recited it, but in your minds and hearts you must keep it ever present, you must repeat it in your beds, recall it in the public squares and not forget it during meals: even when your body is asleep, you must watch over it with your hearts."[55]

Today's Europe suffers the lack of persons in authority who are living witnesses to the truth. Authority is held by morally and intellectually immature journalists and scientists, whose words do not do what they say because they are merely words. Norwid wrote about this pseudo-authority in 1871 to the Polish philosopher August Cieszkowski: "I don't believe today's philosophers. They proclaim systems from their university chairs, but if someone strikes the ground with his rifle or jingles money before them loudly enough, they immediately bow the great mass of their intelligent heads like stalks of grain bending in the wind. There are two specialized fields I recommend studying. They are mainly Homer and the Bible."[56]

Europe is a tree growing out of the Bible and Homer. Its roots reach into heaven and earth. The tree cut off from its roots withers. It is fit to be burned, or can serve as material to produce objects for short-term use. Only a return to the roots can save the dead tree. We must pray for a new life for Europe, for its reason to return to the truth and its will to the good. This is the prayer Plato advises, when he asks God to help the State: "Let us therefore summon God to attend the foundation of the state. May he hear our prayers, and having heard, come graciously and benevolently to help us settle our state and its laws. . . . May he come indeed."[57]

Those who left the paternal home of the true and the good live in the chaos of confused ideas and concepts that are purely artificial, detached from reality. They lose their sovereignty in this chaos, as do society and the State. Escaping the chaos of ideas and concepts involves freeing the

---

55. St. Augustine, Homily 215.1. Cited in Benedict XVI, Apostolic Letter *Motu Proprio Porta fidei*, October 11, 2011, no. 9.

56. Cyprian Norwid to August Cieszkowski, in *Pisma wszystkie*, vol. 9, p. 478.

57. Plato, *Laws* 712b.

Nation and State

State from an economy and a politics that assume the right to make decisions about the human person and society. Cardinal Karol Wojtyła spoke about this when he preached the Spiritual Exercises to Pope Paul VI and the papal household.[58]

Bishop Karol Wojtyła stood up to a State administered by the Communist Party, which decided what was good or evil for its citizens according to its own interests. As Pope, he stood up against the power of the political and economic elite, who basically treated the human person and society in the same way. Both these powers canceled out the difference between true and false, good and evil, in order the more easily to dominate a society. At the inauguration of his pontificate on October 22, 1978, John Paul II cried out to all the individuals and peoples of the earth, "Be not afraid!" Do not be afraid of the lords of the economy and politics, because it is not they who create history. History is created by those who cultivate man, who create a culture rooted in the worship of the Transcendence that is God. People fear the mighty so long as they do not seek salvation in personal communities — in friendships, marriage, family, the nation, and the Church. Europe is caught in talons similar to those which gripped Poland, whose situation Norwid describes clearly in "Song from Our Land":

> From the East — sly lies and obscurantism,
> Cowed obedience and a golden cage,
>   Leprosy, venom and filth.
>
> In the West — glittering lies of knowledge
> Truth's formalism — vacuous interiors
>   And arrogance! . . .
>
> Where the stuff of the brain no longer
> Distracts from the spirit — O West — I, a stupid Slav
>   Await you! . . .
>
> And to you, O East, I state the day of visitation,
> When every moral conscience will fade
>   In your immensity![59]

---

58. John Paul II, *Sign of Contradiction* (New York: Seabury Press, 1979).

59. Cyprian Norwid, *Poesie*, trans. Silvano De Fanti and Giorgio Origlia (Bologna: CSEO, 1981), pp. 55-56.

Scientists will not help Europe to free itself from the grip of lies and truth's formalism. As human beings, they are unable morally to keep pace with the technological progress they themselves have achieved. They have destroyed the unity of *praxis* and *theoria* (contemplation), and have therefore reduced *theoria* to a first step of *praxis*. We should not be surprised that they have surrendered to a politics that, basing itself not on truth but on the effectiveness of opinions, destroys the tie that binds us to reality. The destruction of this bond suppresses the realism that is indispensable for maintaining the human person's spiritual balance. A lack of realism makes society incapable of defending itself against secularization, because he who does not belong to the truth can belong to anything at all. Escape from reality ends in the dictatorship of relativism.

Only prophets and poets can lead Europe out of the land of slavery. Only they can reawaken Europe with the word and the song dictated by faith, hope, and love. Europeans will recover their personal sovereignty when they have created a culture that "cannot be conceived without humanism and wisdom."[60] An *anamnesis*, or remembering, of the true and the good will free them from an insipid scientific mentality, and allow their desire to speak of the stars or ideals indicated by the Latin word *desiderium* (*sidus*, *sideris* means "star"). The human heart desires to be with the stars.

If the European Constitution is not founded on this *desiderium*, the words that are to function as the foundation of the European Union will be like chaff blown away by the wind. Constitutions ought to be written by friends of the truth revealed in man. They ought not to be written by people like Valéry Giscard d'Estaing, who assured the Pope that he wanted to mention Christian values in the text of the European Constitution. But others were opposed and Giscard d'Estaing made no mention of any such values. To Professor Joseph Weiler,[61] who observed that he was the main author of the text, Giscard d'Estaing merely responded with a smile, "How malicious you are, Mr. Weiler!"

Europe cannot be treated as one would treat a division of soldiers. Every State, and therefore also Europe as a whole, arises not from a mass of individuals, says Aristotle, but from a union of human beings "differing

---

60. John Paul II, address to the participants in the Plenary Assembly of the Pontifical Academy of Sciences, October 28, 1994.

61. Joseph H. H. Weiler, professor of law and European Union at New York University School of Law and president of the European University Institute, known for his work on European integration.

in kind. A collection of persons all alike does not constitute a state. For a city is not the same thing as a league."⁶² A military formation is a grouping of geometric figures designed by human beings. Man, on the other hand, receives his form — his identity — from God.

Does the ideal exist, from which States can draw their own life, bound up as it is with the identity assigned to them as a task? In other words, does an ideal human being and an ideal State exist anywhere? Such a State "exists in theory," says Socrates in Plato's *Republic*, "for I don't think it exists anywhere on earth. But perhaps ... there is a model of it in heaven, for anyone who wants to look at it and to make himself its citizen on the strength of what he sees. It makes no difference whether it is or ever will be somewhere."⁶³ Beauty and the moral conscience keep the memory alive in us of stars or ideals that are found only in heaven.

The wealth Europe enjoys is by no means ideal. Unfortunately, Europe's wealth and misery succeed one another, since this wealth is not transfigured by the person's presence to other persons. Europe's wealth is a trap, a miserable wealth in which the *parousia* of the person does not take place. In this misery, gifts are like the wooden horse the Greeks left at the gates of Troy. In a famous line of Virgil's *Aeneid*, Laocoön warns the Trojans, *"Timeo Danaos et dona ferentes!"* ["I fear the Greeks, even those bearing gifts"].⁶⁴ As in the Trojan horse, the gifts that the European States make to one another contain soldiers ready to continue their diplomatic efforts under the guise of war.

Plato had all this in mind when he wrote that politics and economics must not be carried out by those whom he defined as "illegitimate." They "love the truth when it bathes them in its light; they hate it when it proves them wrong."⁶⁵ Truth flees from "illegitimate" sons, for they enjoy themselves at its expense, staining it with their egoism and childish interests.

> The truths proclaimed by egoism — are they enduring?
> The truths proclaimed by self-interest — are they whole?⁶⁶

---

62. Aristotle, *Politics* 1261a, trans. H. Rackham, in *Aristotle in 23 Volumes*, vol. 21 (Cambridge, MA: Harvard University Press, 1944).

63. Plato, *Republic* 592a-b.

64. Virgil, *Aeneid* 2.49.

65. St. Augustine, *Confessions* 10.23: *"Amant veritatem lucentem, oderunt eam redarguentem."*

66. Cyprian Norwid, "Do L. Nabielaka: Post-Scriptum," in *Pisma wszystkie*, vol. 2, p. 251.

Man will never be at home in a State that is "idiotic" in the Greek sense of this word. Such a State does not concern itself with the unity of its citizens, which originates in persons who are so present to one another that one gives his life for all, and all for one. Where there is nothing for which to die, there is also nothing for which it is worth living. It is worth living and dying only for the truth that "happens" in the human person. People attached themselves to John Paul II and formed the Church around him not so much on account of his words, but on account of who he was — that is, for the truth that "happened" in him.

Europe lacks great statesmen, in whom the event of the truth of man and of society can take place. Politicians have become boring and banal. They seek ephemeral success without looking toward a future victory. As Plato writes in the *Laws*,

> Where the ruler of the state is not a god but a mortal, people have no respite from toil and misfortune.... [W]e should run our public and our private life, our homes and our cities, in obedience to what little spark of immortality lies in us, and dignify these edicts of reason with the name of "law." But take an individual man, or an oligarchy, or even a democracy, that lusts in its heart for pleasure and demands to have its fill of everything it wants — the perpetually unsatisfied victim of an evil greed that attacks it like the plague — well ... if a power like that controls a state or an individual and rides roughshod over the laws, it's impossible to escape disaster.[67]

Asphyxiated by the French Enlightenment, Europe entrusts itself to a reason that brandishes the words "liberty, equality, fraternity." But these words have been detached from the "vine" (cf. John 15:5) and so are dead; they cannot express the inestimable values for which it is worth living and dying.[68] No technical reform that we invent can bring Europe back to health. The only thing that can do this is the rebirth of Europeans, their conversion to the stars or ideals of which their *desiderium* speaks (*desiderium* is derived from *sidus, -eris*, star). Only when we aim at these ideals are we defended by Transcendence and saved from relativism. The only thing that can bring Europe back to health is the freedom revealed in Socrates' words to the Athenian jurors — "Gentlemen of the jury, I am

---

67. Plato, *Laws* 713e and 714a.
68. Cf. John Paul II, *Memory and Identity*, chap. 18.

Nation and State

grateful and I am your friend, but I will obey the god rather than you"[69] — and in Peter and John's reply to the Sanhedrin: "Whether it is right in the sight of God to listen to you rather than to God, you must judge" (Acts 4:19). Every technical invention fails to oppose what is merely human in the name of what is more than human, since it does not elevate the human person to what is more than human.

Politicians who neither listen to the human person nor know how to read the Decalogue written in him will obey only their own ideas and the cry of the masses, rather than the dignity of the person. This does not mean that the State must take the side of the Church or grant her privileges. Truth and love do not need privileges. They are self-sufficient. The Church of truth and of love must be a living sign that reminds every Pharaoh of the words of the Lord: "Let my people go, that they may hold a feast to me in the wilderness" (Exod. 5:1). Do not force the people to adore your gods, for the Lord is infinitely greater than they. The State does not have the power to say this to itself, so it needs to be "helped" in a way that befits not so much itself but its citizens.

The Lord is adored in the desert, where "having" decreases, but "being" — that is, the "I am" — increases in all those who cross the desert. Journeying toward the promised truth and the promised good in order to become themselves, they live in so great a hope.

John Paul II never sought to obtain privileges for ecclesiastical institutions from the State. He never asked politicians to preach. All he asked of them was that they seek the truth and do the good. When one of them lied to him, he laughed to the man's face. After his encounter with the Soviet Minister of Foreign Affairs, Andrei Gromyko,[70] I asked the Pope how it was possible to speak with someone like that. "He spun tales about the great freedom that the Soviet regime had granted to the Church," he said. "And what did you say?" I asked. "Nothing," he answered. "I just looked at him and laughed!" I think that Gromyko had a hard time continuing to drown himself with lies, even though he was a very good liar.

John Paul II did everything possible to conquer evil with good. He never lost hope when evil seemed to triumph. He knew that evil would never conquer the good, but would only place it in greater relief. Even in the *anus mundi* that were the Nazi extermination camps and the Soviet

---

69. Plato, *Apology* 29d.
70. A Soviet statesman who served as minister of foreign affairs (1957-1985) and chairman of the Presidium of the Supreme Soviet (1985-1988).

gulags, the truth and the good conquered in people of the caliber of Maximilian Kolbe, Edith Stein, or the great Russian theologian and scientist Pawel Florenski. The true and the good reveal their power in every paschal event that unites man to the Pasch of the God-man, even when man is unaware of it. John Paul II knew well that the freedom brought by the true and the good is a difficult freedom. We must continually fight for it in order to be able to *be* it in our turn for others. He who does not become a gift has no one to whom he can turn. He lives in misery.

The fate of man is decided in people who become a gift for others. It is in them that the kind of history not reported in newspapers is accomplished. In them, the world returns to the point where it went astray, abandoning the Origin and End that are the True and the Good. These people are the only realists in this world. Europe lacks realists, it lacks people who are present to themselves and to others. For this reason, it lacks the strength to be reborn. Europe cannot live on economics, but on people who, as holy realists, offer themselves for the common good. "The immolated spirit is the light of the nation."[71] This is the freedom for which we must fight.

The "No!" that those who offer themselves speak to those carrying poison risks the lives of free men, who are accused of folly. But without risk there is not even a game, let alone life. In *Thus Spoke Zarathustra*, Nietzsche describes the earth and man, which have become "small":

> "A little poison now and then: that makes for agreeable dreams. And much poison in the end, for an agreeable death.
>
> "... One no longer becomes poor or rich: both require too much exertion. Who still wants to rule? Who obey? Both require too much exertion.
>
> "No shepherd and one herd! Everybody wants the same, everybody is the same: whoever feels different goes voluntarily into a madhouse."[72]

Those who are "refined" do not tolerate "madmen." Yet it is the "madmen," not those who think themselves "normal," who come to society's aid.

This is what Antisthenes of Athens had in mind when he made himself

---

71. Juliusz Słowacki, "Zawisza Czarny," in *Dzieła*, vol. 10 (Wrocław: Wydawn. Zakładu Narodowego im. Ossolińskich, 1959), p. 7.

72. Friedrich Nietzsche, *Thus Spoke Zarathustra*, trans. Walter Kaufman (New York: Penguin, 1978), pp. 17-18.

the laughingstock of his fellow citizens. He advised them to be "refined" enough to vote for the transformation of donkeys into horses, against the "madmen" who had the courage to live, think, and speak differently. It is not easy to live in States in which politicians seek to turn donkeys into horses. Plato writes, "Only a god ... would be entitled to insist that this view is correct — there are so many conflicting opinions."[73] Only a god is sure of the truth. If people who are like gods do not appear in Europe, it will become mere material that can be made into anything at all. Europeans will vote for the transformation not only of donkeys into horses, but into men and vice versa.

Karol Wojtyła believed that history will not "flow against the current of conscience,"[74] thanks also to a few people who keep watch over it. "Vigil is the word of the Lord and the word of the People, which we continually receive anew."[75] Those who keep vigil risk their lives. The shot fired at John Paul II on May 13, 1981, almost cost him his life.

History will not "flow against the current of conscience," even if history were to be identified with God and the State made an idol. The State is not enough for man. Politicians are not enough, who insinuate themselves by force between man's reason and the truth, between his will and the good. It is not enough for a person to be a loyal citizen, that is, to be a politically correct weathervane. The faiths of States change direction, but the mechanism of political obedience remains the same. Hegel deified history. He was an enthusiast first of the French Revolution, then of Napoleon ("reason on a horse"); finally, he bowed before the Prussian State. Luckily, he did not live long enough to see Hitler or Stalin. St. Augustine's admonition in *The City of God* does not cease to be relevant. The saint wrote that States without God degenerate into gangs of political scoundrels who take advantage of the momentum of generations of the just. Despite this, they move toward an inevitable defeat. Gangs of political scoundrels do not listen to the voice of conscience — or they pretend they do not hear. They do not contemplate beauty. Their members fix their gaze only on their bosses and listen attentively only to their voice.

Today's Europe is like the Grand Inquisitor in Dostoyevsky's *The Brothers Karamazov*. His heart trembles at Christ's kiss, but he nonethe-

---

73. Plato, *Laws* 641d.
74. Karol Wojtyła, "Thinking My Country: Thinking My Country I Return to the Tree," p. 148.
75. Karol Wojtyła, "Thinking My Country: Thinking My Country I Return to the Tree," p. 149.

less persists in his own ideas, which lack prophecy, priesthood, and kingly freedom. The political and economic vicissitudes of Europe, which advance in the direction of the unknown, suffocate John Paul II's cry: "I, John Paul II . . . cry out with love to you, ancient Europe: Find yourself again. Be yourself. Rediscover your origins. Revive your roots. Return to living the authentic values that made your history glorious. . . . Reconstruct your spiritual unity. . . . Do not take such pride in your conquests that you forget their possible negative consequences. Do not be depressed at the quantitative loss of your greatness in the world, or at the social and cultural crises in your midst. You can still be a beacon of civilization and a stimulus toward progress for the world. Other continents look to you; from you, they await the response that St. James gave to Christ: 'I can.'"[76]

Will Europe manage to reach the peaks on which realism and sanctity form a single whole?[77] Will it realize that in order to be itself, it must transcend political and economic circumstances? Since it does not wish to accept the truth, however, Norwid articulates the problem Europe faces if it still wants to be itself:

> We mustn't think that it is possible
> To be at once democratic, Godless and faithless
> (Something that has never been from the beginning of this old world!)
> Or that there can be martyrdom
>   without confession.
>
> We mustn't bow to Circumstance
> And make Truth wait at the door,
> Selling laurel wreaths to old acquaintances,
> Thinking: the drums will drown out
> the rhythm of history.[78]

Will Europe be democratic enough to elect as administrators, not lovers of administration,[79] but rather servants of the common good?

---

76. John Paul II, Europeistic act in Santiago de Compostela, Spain, November 9, 1982, no. 4.

77. John Paul II, Europeistic act in Santiago de Compostela, Spain, November 9, 1982, no. 4.

78. Cyprian Norwid, "LXIX. Początek broszury politycznej . . . ," in *Pisma wszystkie*, vol. 2, p. 99.

79. Cf. Plato, *Republic* 521b.

These questions are to some extent linked to the question, "What will remain in our personal and social life after the great event that was the pontificate of John Paul II?" Will our answer do justice to his teaching, which was present among us? Monuments and commemorative stones doubtless have importance and value, but Christ did not call Peter so that what might remain of him were memories in stone. Christ called Peter so that he might strengthen our confidence even in the restlessness of our hearts, which point us to the Source of the true, the good, and the beautiful. In the desire of our restless heart, we perceive the call that opens the path for us to a daily "new evangelization." We respond to the call inadequately because of our weakness. And we are weak because we are too rich to be free as Socrates was free. He said to the judges who condemned him to death, "I . . . have a convincing witness that I speak the truth, my poverty."[80] We are too rich, and so we go away sad in our hearts when we are called to journey toward the truth and to change our life for its sake (cf. Luke 18:23).

I am ever more convinced that the human person journeys toward the truth to which his own heart points him to the extent that he is a mystic and a poet — in other words, to the extent that he is prophetic, priestly, and kingly. Both John Paul II and the Servant of God Bishop Jan Pietraszko were such men; they showed me this truth with their lives.

Three weeks before the death of Hans Urs von Balthasar, the Swiss theologian said something to me in a private conversation that helped me to understand better the person and the act of John Paul II. "They say that I created something new in theology," Balthasar said. "That's not true. I didn't do anything new. Everything that I wrote, I found in the poets or heard from Adrienne von Speyr. Now, reading the texts of John Paul II, I see that I would have to change a lot of things in my theological thinking. Unfortunately, I'm too old and I don't have the strength to be able do this." When, after Balthasar's death, I repeated the great theologian's words to John Paul II, he asked me, "He really said this?" I said, "Yes, but unfortunately he's not here anymore, so. . . ." "That doesn't matter," interrupted the Pope. "It matters to me that he said it."

The poet and the mystic journey along the path of difficult beauty, the *via pulchritudinis*, which is also a sorrowful path, a *via crucis*. They ask questions about the truth, and also wait for it. Ready to give their lives for the truth, they are free with the freedom of prophets, priests, and kings.

80. Plato, *Apology* 31c.

Discovering the Human Person

Karol Wojtyła walked this path. His questions about the truth of man were transfigured in the prayer that finds one of its many expressions in his poem, "Song of the Inexhaustible Sun":

> I beseech you, Lord, leave me
> and my fallible thoughts,
> put me not to the test of weakness,
> the test of incapacity.
>
> For there is no gratitude
> that can embrace infinity,
> no heart that can encircle You
> with the sun's ring of red.
>
> If the heart enclosed the world,
> and the world went up in flames,
> even if I spent myself,
> nothing I could give, I know.
>
> Yet day by day You multiply
> my feeble ineffectual lot,
> surrendering your infinity
> to my fallible thought.
>
> . . . .
>
> Forgive my thought, Lord, for not loving enough.
> My love is so mind-manacled, forgive that, Lord.[81]

---

81. Karol Wojtyła, "Song of the Hidden God: Song of the Inexhaustible Sun," in *Place Within*, pp. 23-25.

www.ingramcontent.com/pod-product-compliance
Lightning Source LLC
Chambersburg PA
CBHW021811220426
43662CB00006B/270